FROM CLICHÉ TO ARCHETYPE

FROM **C**LICHÉ

MARSHALL McLUHAN

with Wilfred Watson

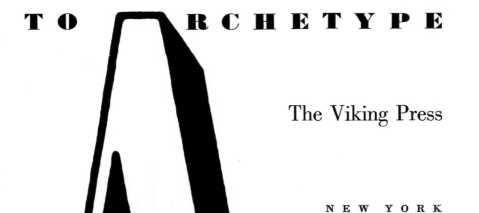

TO ARCHETYPE

The Viking Press

NEW YORK

First published in 1970 by The Viking Press, Inc.
625 Madison Avenue, New York, N.Y. 10022

Published simultaneously in Canada by
The Macmillan Company of Canada Limited

SBN 670–33093–0

Library of Congress catalog card number: 74–83257

Printed in U.S.A.

ACKNOWLEDGMENTS

Cambridge University Press: Excerpts from *The Forms of Action at Common Law* by F. W. Maitland.

Chatto and Windus Ltd. and Q. D. Leavis: Excerpts from *Fiction and the Reading Public* by Q. D. Leavis.

Constable & Company Limited: Excerpt from *Words and Idioms* by Logan Pearsall Smith.

Dodd, Mead & Company, Inc., and Miss D. Collins and J. M. Dent & Sons: "The Donkey" by G. K. Chesterton. From *The Collected Poems of G. K. Chesterton* and from *The Wild Knight and Other Poems*. Copyright 1932 by Dodd, Mead & Company, Inc. Copyright renewed.

Doubleday & Company, Inc.: Excerpts from *The Silent Language* by Edward T. Hall. Copyright © 1959 by Edward T. Hall.

Faber and Faber Ltd. and Mrs. Valerie Eliot, the copyright owner: Excerpt from "*Ulysses*, Order and Myth" by T. S. Eliot. First published in *The Dial*, 1923.

Farrar, Straus & Giroux, Inc.: Excerpts from *Against Interpretation* by Susan Sontag. Copyright © 1964, 1965 by Susan Sontag.

W. H. Freeman and Company, and Scientific American, Inc.: Excerpt from "Movements of the Eye" by E. Llewellyn Thomas from the August 1968 issue of *Scientific American*. Copyright © 1968 by Scientific American, Inc. All rights reserved.

Funk & Wagnalls: Excerpts from *The Eclipse of the Intellectual* by Elémire Zolla, translated by Raymond Rosenthal. Translation copyright © 1968 by Funk & Wagnalls. All rights reserved. *Eclissi Dell' Intellettuale*, Copyright 1956 by Valentino Bompiano, Milan. *Volgarità E Dolore*, Copyright 1962 by Valentino Bompiano, Milan.

Grey Advertising, Inc.: Advertisement for "Celanese Arnel" in *The New York Times Magazine*.

Grove Press, Inc.: Excerpts from *The Bald Soprano* from *Four Plays* by Eugene Ionesco, translated by Donald M. Allen. Copyright © 1956, 1965 by Grove Press, Inc.

Grove Press, Inc., and Jonathan Cape Ltd.: Excerpt from *Problems of the Theatre*, an essay, and *The Marriage of Mr. Mississippi*, a play, by Friedrich Dürrenmatt, translated by Gerhard Nellhaus. Copyright © 1957 by Peter Schifferli, Verlags AG 'Die Arche'; Copyright © 1958 by Gerhard Nellhaus.

Harcourt Brace Jovanovich, Inc.: Excerpts from Frame's original text in *Montaigne: A Biography* by Donald M. Frame. Harcourt Brace Jovanovich, Inc., and Faber and Faber Ltd.: Extracts from "The Love Song of Alfred Prufrock," "The Waste Land," "Whispers of Immortality," and "Sweeney Erect" by T. S. Eliot. From *Collected Poems 1909–1962* by T. S. Eliot. Harcourt Brace Jovanovich, Inc., and Chatto and Windus Ltd. and William Empson: "The Fire Sermon" by William Empson. From *Collected Poems of William Empson*. Copyright 1949 by William Empson. Extract from "Legal Fiction" by William Empson. From *Collected Poems of William Empson*.

Harvard University Press: Excerpts from *Preface to Plato* by Eric Havelock. Harvard University Press and The Loeb Classical Library: Excerpts from *Institutio Oratoria* by Quintilian translated by H. E. Butler.

FROM CLICHÉ TO ARCHETYPE

ABSURD, THEATER OF THE

Bergman makes it possible for the mass-man to entertain the illusion that he is meditating, racking his brain.

"A good movie is better than a bad play or a bad book."

This commonplace is like a loose rock; lifting it exposes the rot and vermin underneath. It is Robinsonism, that is, a deduction flowing from an hypothesis of complete isolation (as on Robinson Crusoe's island) applied to a reality in which there is no isolation. In the same way, one says: "Better an ugly, ignoble woman than masturbation," "Better a good photograph than a bad portrait," "Better an attractive hallucination than an ugly reality." The basic fallacy of these statements consists in presupposing a nonexistent coercion to choose.

—Elémire Zolla, *The Eclipse of the Intellectual*

Impovernment of the booble by the bauble for the bubble.

—James Joyce, *Finnegans Wake*

To the theatergoers of the 1950s the plays of Samuel Beckett and Eugene Ionesco seemed something strange and wonderful. Those who were at all familiar with contemporary literature should not have been startled because what was really a cult of the absurd had begun very early with Baudelaire. Critics have since traced to Joyce and to Jarry's *Ubu Roi,* which was produced in the last decade of the nineteenth century, the beginnings of the absurdist theater movement. Camus was looked to as the journalist of this cult of the absurd which includes much of the plainer, intense nineteenth century, much twentieth-century art, Magritte, Breton and the Surrealists, cubism, and Dadaism.

> Ionesco wrote his first drama in 1948, *The Bald Soprano*, as a tragedy of language, using the stereotyped dialogues he found in the Assimil-method primer from which he was learning English. As he studied the clichés in this exercise book— "There are seven days in the week, it costs too much, I don't have the right change, the room is too warm, where is the W.C."—he felt the text changing under his eyes: it began to ferment, he says, and he saw that these automatic colloquies represented very well the collapse of our daily lives. We go on speaking as if we were stricken by some sort of amnesia. So Ionesco wrote his anti-play in which the Smiths and the Martins talk, talk, talk the babble that sounds, when one is able really to hear it, appallingly like what one hears at any cocktail party. The characters disintegrate into the jargon that serves us as a way of life.
>
> —Wylie Sypher, *Loss of the Self in Modern Literature and Art*

The Smiths and the Browns were so identical that at the end of the play the curtain falls on the Browns who are repeating the opening dialogue of the play which had been assigned to the Smiths. Ionesco originally put all these idiomatic English clichés into literary French which presented the English in the most absurd aspect possible.

> MRS. SMITH: There, it's nine o'clock. We've drunk the soup, and eaten the fish and chips, and the English salad. The children have drunk English water. We've eaten well this evening. That's because we live in the suburbs of London and because our name is Smith.
>
> MR. SMITH (*continues to read, clicks his tongue*).
>
> MRS. SMITH: Potatoes are very good fried in fat; the salad oil was not rancid. The oil from the grocer at the corner is better quality than the oil from the grocer across the

4

street. It is even better than the oil from the grocer at the bottom of the street. However, I prefer not to tell them that their oil is bad.

—*The Bald Soprano*

The Bald Soprano of this play is a figure of the long-haired musical world, a figure of eternal resonating garbage where the usefulness of art and the usefulness of garbage become interchangeable. Ionesco's absurd is the unconscious brought up to daylight inspection.

Pascal, in the seventeenth century, tells us that the heart has many reasons of which the head knows nothing. The Theater of the Absurd is essentially a communicating to the head of some of the silent languages of the heart which in two or three hundred years it had tried to forget all about. In the seventeenth-century world the languages of the heart were pushed down into the unconscious by the dominant print cliché. In the contemporary world the unconscious is being retrieved and brought up into daylight awareness. This is done for both private and corporate psyche. Edward T. Hall in *The Silent Language* reveals many of the nonverbal gestures by which whole cultures communicate. He tells us, for example, that an eight-inch interval between speakers is normal and friendly in the Arab world. Beyond eight inches it is not easy to smell one's interlocutor. When the Arab can no longer smell his interlocutor, he stops talking and begins gesticulating. A rather similar incident occurs in *The Bald Soprano* when the Smiths and the Browns, in the midst of a painful English silence, meet each other for the first time. The dialogue goes: "Sniff . . . sniff . . . snifff . . . sniff . . . snifff . . ."

Ionesco particularly cultivates the art of the verbal cliché, and he uses the verbal cliché to probe one of the most fascinating phenomena of our age and that is the way in which the Western mind is changing its mind. His characteristic effect is a sort of shudder, or *frisson*, not unlike the metaphysical shudder which George Williamson detected in much seventeenth-century metaphysical verse. It is probable that the metaphysical shudder was related to the shift from oral to written, and it is likely that the

5

absurdist *frisson* is a seismic recorder of a global shudder from new environmental technologies. The extremely mobile individual consciousness of the print-oriented man now reverses into the tribal inertia of multi-consciousness. It is rather similar to what happens when countries demobilize at the end of a major war.

Anyone first approaching the Theater of the Absurd might well ask such questions as: "Why is the favorite mode of this theater called 'tragic farce,' as it is by Ionesco?" A tentative answer is given by Friedrich Dürrenmatt in "Problems of the Theatre":

> Tragedy presupposes guilt, despair, moderation, lucidity, vision, a sense of responsibility. In the Punch-and-Judy show of our century, in this back-sliding of the white race, there are no more guilty and also, no responsible men. It is always, "We couldn't help it" and "We didn't really want that to happen." And indeed, things happen without anyone in particular being responsible for them. Everything is dragged along and everyone gets caught somewhere in the sweep of events. We are all collectively guilty, collectively bogged down in the sins of our fathers and of our forefathers. We are the offspring of children. That is our misfortune, but not our guilt: guilt can exist only as a personal achievement, as a religious deed. Comedy alone is suitable for us. Our world has led to the grotesque as well as to the atom bomb, and so it is a world like that of Hieronymus Bosch whose apocalyptic paintings are also grotesque. But the grotesque is only a way of expressing in a tangible manner, of making us perceive physically the paradoxical, the form of the unformed, the face of a world without face; and just as in our thinking today we seem to be unable to do without the concept of the paradox, so also in art, and in our world which at times seems still to exist only because the atom bomb exists: out of fear of the bomb.
>
> But the tragic is still possible even if pure tragedy is not. We can achieve the tragic out of comedy. We can bring it forth as a frightening moment, as an abyss that opens suddenly; indeed, many of Shakespeare's tragedies are already really comedies out of which the tragic arises.

The Bald Soprano and the
Frigean Anatomy of a Metamorphosis

In *The Bald Soprano* the Fire Chief waits to ensure that all the fires are "turned off."

> FIRE CHIEF: "The Headcold." My brother-in-law had, on the paternal side, a first cousin whose maternal uncle had a father-in-law whose paternal grandfather had married as his second wife a young native whose brother he had met on one of his travels, a girl of whom he was enamored and by whom he had a son who married an intrepid lady pharmacist who was none other than the niece of an unknown fourth-class petty officer of the Royal Navy and whose adopted father had an aunt who spoke Spanish fluently and who was, perhaps, one of the granddaughters of an engineer who died young, . . .

MR. MARTIN: I knew that third wife, if I'm not mistaken. She ate chicken sitting on a hornet's nest.

FIRE CHIEF: It's not the same one.

MRS. SMITH: Shh!

FIRE CHIEF: As I was saying . . . whose third wife was the daughter of the best midwife in the region and who, early left a widow . . .

MR. SMITH: Like my wife.

FIRE CHIEF: . . . Had married a glazier who was full of life and who had had, by the daughter of a station master, a child who had burned his bridges . . .

MRS. SMITH: His britches?

MR. MARTIN: No his bridge game.

FIRE CHIEF: And had married an oyster woman, whose father had a brother, mayor of a small town, who had taken as his wife a blonde schoolteacher, whose cousin, a fly fisherman . . .

MR. MARTIN: A fly by night?

FIRE CHIEF: . . . Had married another blonde schoolteacher,

7

named Marie, too, whose brother was married to another
Marie, also a blonde schoolteacher . . .

MR. SMITH: Since she's blonde, she must be Marie.

FIRE CHIEF: . . . And whose father had been reared in Canada by an old woman who was the niece of a priest whose
grandmother, occasionally in the winter, like everyone else,
caught a cold. . . .

Assimil-like phrase books for studying foreign languages were
also everyday resources for James Joyce (who taught in the Berlitz
School of Languages). His *Wake* raises the verbal stereotype to
archetypal awareness as does Eliot's Sweeney's "I've gotta use
words when I talk to you."

> But O felicitous culpability, sweet bad cess to you for an
> archetypt!
>
> —*Finnegans Wake*

The fall or scrapping of a culture world puts us all into the same
archetypal cesspool. As a precursor of the Theater of the Absurd,
Joyce exposes the archetypal unconscious as an absurd landscape
of one world burrowing on another.

Jan Kott, in *Shakespeare Our Contemporary*, is prepared to re-
vise Shakespearean tragedies like *Othello* and *King Lear* into
tragic farces. Peter Brook, an admirer of this Polish teacher of
theater, directs *King Lear* according to Jan Kott's recipe for tragic
farce. It would seem likely that once again, as in the seventeenth
century, Shakespeare, in tragedy, if slanted in an absurdist way,
can be used to explore changing modes of consciousness.

Another question concerns the fondness of absurdist writers for
treating their characters in a situation of impasse like that of
the four people in Sartre's *No Exit*, or those in Beckett's *Waiting
for Godot*. Hugh Kenner has commented on this feature of the
absurd. In his study *The Stoic Comedians*, he has even called
Samuel Beckett, as a son of James Joyce, a dramatist of the
impasse.

Why are Beckett, Joyce, Ionesco, Picasso, and many other absurdist expatriates alienated from their own countries? One might
venture the answer that the universal human condition today in a

8

period of rapid innovation is necessarily that of alienation. Every culture now rides on the back of every other culture. Joyce's *Exiles* is explicitly a drama of the absurd. This piggybacking of languages and cultures appears in the verbal index of *Finnegans Wake* as much as in the painting of Picasso. The absurd is not without its high spirits, even in tragic farce, where the range goes from the fun of Ionesco to the *misérabilisme* of Bernard Buffet.

Another question: What is the relation between the electrically illuminated Ibscenist realism (Ibscenist nansence, *Finnegans Wake*) and absurdist theater? We can think of electricity in the modern world as a form of retrieval which brings back the dour realism of Ibsen in a comic overexaggeration in a comic life. It is a demonstrable fact that if you play Ibsen in the theater with reduced lighting values, you secure the intended realistic effect. But if you turn up the lights to high intensity, it converts into comic archetype, or archetype which is "camp" or comic, depending on the emphasis. You might observe that *The Penguin Dictionary of Theatre*, in its article on the Theater of the Absurd, sees this movement as coming to an end in 1960. This may be so. Nevertheless, critics still write of absurdist elements in contemporary plays. A fairly large number of studies have been devoted to defining this movement, with such titles as Brustein's *The Theatre of Revolt* and Wellwarth's *Theater of Protest and Paradox*.

Absurdist theater then shifts after 1960 into the theater of blood and cruelty which Arnaud called for in several manifestoes which he inserted into his book *The Theatre and Its Double* (1937). Arnaud is essentially archetypalizing. At that time his recipe for theater found no takers, and it didn't do so until Peter Weiss's *The Persecution and Assassination of Jean-Paul Marat as Performed by the Inmates of the Asylum of Charenton under the Direction of the Marquis de Sade* had turned his Arnaudian formula into cliché probe of the violences and dislocations of the multiconscious global village of 1963 and after.

Since Sputnik and the satellites, the planet is enclosed in a man-made environment that ends "Nature" and turns the globe into a repertory theater to be programed. Shakespeare at the Globe mentioning "All the world's a stage, and all the men and women

9

merely players" (*As You Like It*, Act II, Scene 7) has been justi-
fied by recent events in ways that would have struck him as entirely
paradoxical. The results of living inside a proscenium arch of
satellites is that the young now accept the public spaces of the earth
as role-playing areas. Sensing this, they adopt costumes and roles
and are ready to "do their thing" everywhere. Shakespeare's
global cliché about the world as a stage was caught up by T. S.
Eliot in "O O O O that Shakespeherian Rag—/It's so elegant/
So intelligent." The "rag" or syncopated jazz catches up the theme
of the new global unity created in the twenties by the international
acceptance of jazz. It "cocks a snoot" at the rag-and-bone shop of
the global waste land of Shakespeare & Co., or the international
translations of the Shakespearean archetypes.

_____

ANESTHESIA

Not only does the cinema rob the daydream of its confused, evanescent aura, dispersing the mist to reveal very clear ghosts similar to living men yet of greater stature, not only does it silence the voice of reality by saying "I can do without you," but society, too, gradually becomes incapable of giving the lie to the somnambulist. At one time a young man zigzagging down the street, wriggling his hips and mumbling "bee boh, boh, boh, bee bee boh boh" or grimacing with gritted teeth and narrowed eyes, would have been mocked and so awakened. Today he encounters no opposition or criticism; everybody recognizes and understands the dream in which he is immersed, the dream made respectable by industry.

—Elémire Zolla, *The Eclipse of the Intellectual*

Since Sputnik put the globe in a "proscenium arch," and the global village has been transformed into a global theater, the result, quite literally, is the use of public space for "doing one's thing." A planet parenthesized by a man-made environment no longer offers any directions or goals to nation or individual. The world itself has become a probe. "Snooping with intent to creep" or "casing everybody else's joint" has become a major activity. As the main business of the world becomes espionage, secrecy becomes the basis of wealth, as with magic in a tribal society. Perhaps this is not the only latest form of cliché probe but merely the largest and most perceptible.

It is just when people are all engaged in snooping on themselves and one another that they become anesthetized to the whole process. Tranquilizers and anesthetics, private and corporate, become the largest business in the world just as the world is attempting to maximize every form of alert. Sound-light shows, as new cliché, are in effect mergers, retrievers of the tribal condition. It is a state that has already overtaken private enterprise, as individual businesses form into massive conglomerates. As information itself becomes the largest business in the world, data banks know more about individual people than the people do themselves. The more the data banks record about each one of us, the less we exist.

The old hardware city, congested and polluted, appeals to many as a psychedelic experience. Urban renewal is a macroform of surgery, made possible by the anesthesia of town planners and publicity barrages that numb all public awareness. The negative clichés of public anesthesia prepare the patient for the surgery of the wreckers and the engineers. The convalescence, or the real disease, comes after the probe and the slicing of the thruways and the high-rise transplants.

The negative clichés of anesthesia demonstrated by the public media permit the wrecking and clearance and transplanting of psyche and population in the new wasteland or city. "I saw the best minds of my generation . . . looking for an angry fix" (Allen Ginsberg).

"The Love Song of J. Alfred Prufrock" opens with the archetypal anesthetic of the romantic landscape: "Let us go then, you and I, when the evening is spread out against the sky." The second image is that of the positive cliché or probe: "Like a patient etherised upon a table."

The Oriental world has, on the whole, tried to anesthetize itself against the inputs of sensation because of its thousands of years of knowledge of the experiential effects of the inputs. The West, in contrast, has tried to maximize the sensational inputs and to minimize the experiential effects. It is useful to have a shorthand for this pattern of input and response: SI/SC—sensory input or impact and sensory closure or involvement. Today the roles of East and West seem to be shifting. The Orient is more inclined today to give the SI side of things a go, while the West, undergoing

13

retribalization, may appear to be already satiated with involvement and participation of SC.

The outer trip has been specialist and Western. The inner trip has been echological and Oriental. Both kinds of trips are cliché-probes. Each has its own methods and preferences of retrieval from the rag-and-bone shop of past experience. The outer trip prefers to retrieve antiquities or archetypes. The inner trip prefers the probing cliché world of the module.

There is a fascinating example in Milton's *Paradise Lost* of the process of intellectual anesthesia. Milton's problem, which is that of orthodox theology, is to explain how Satan, who has supreme created intelligence, should immediately be able to intuit the results of any sin. Therefore the problem is: how can he be said to commit sin and be of high order of intelligence? Milton solves this problem wittily by showing how Satan uses language to obscure his thinking. This process characterizes Satan's speeches to Beelzebub in Book I of *Paradise Lost*:

14

> "If thou beest he; But O how fall'n! how chang'd
> From him, who in the happy Realms of Light
> Clothed with transcendent brightness didst outshine
> Myriads though bright: If he, whom mutual league,
> United thoughts and counsels, equal hope,
> And hazard in the Glorious Enterprize,
> Joynd with me once, now misery hath joynd
> In equal ruin: into what Pit thou seest . . ."

Here Satan clearly recognizes the situation. He is still lying prone on the deeps of Hell. He is not even erect but half floating, half submerged. Flat on his back he turns, rolling his eyes, and looks at his colleagues. As the speech goes on, he comes to confuse his mind so much that he can at the very end of the passage refer to:

> ". . . our grand Foe,
> Who now triumphs, and in th' excess of joy
> Sole reigning holds the Tyranny of Heav'n."

In these last two or three lines Satan has completely obscured to himself the fact of his subordination to God as created Being to uncreated Being, and he has forgotten the defeat which had been inflicted upon him, of which he was conscious at the beginning of the speech. That group of archetypalists who consider the linguistic form to be a recurring pattern of literary experience describe what is antithetic to the cliché as probe.

The conventional idea of cliché as anesthetic should be contrasted to the archetype as inducing somnambulism. Textbook cliché ("as green as grass," "quick as a fox") may at any moment be sharpened into probe, e.g., "far-away pastures look green," "the grass is always greener on the other fellow," or "crazy like a fox." In contrast, the Northrop Frye definition of archetype is: "A symbol, usually an image, which recurs often enough in literature to be recognizable as an element of one's literary experience as a whole." It doesn't matter that in the phrase "as a whole" Frye is using textbook cliché, since he is insisting that the archetypal experience is a pleasing form of somnambulism.

In B. M. Hinkle's Introduction to Jung's *Psychology of the Unconscious* she mentions the stages by which hypnosis led Freud to the discovery of the unconscious. She omits to mention that hypnosis had first been used by Freud as a medical technique of anesthesia for surgery—operation archetype.

Jurgen Thorwald gives further data about Freud's experiments with drugs—from insensibility to psychedeliciousness:

> Freud trickled a few drops of cocaine solution on his gum, without explaining the nature of his panacea. Next day he again encountered Koller, who asked the nature of the medicine. Freud explained, and invited him, as he had done others, to participate in the experiments. Koller promptly acceded and for several weeks took cocaine along with Freud. Both men measured their physical strength and the degree to which it was increased by cocaine. They observed that cocaine induced warmth, deepened respiration, and increased the blood pressure. During this time however, neither man commented on the local anaesthetic effect of cocaine in the mouth.

The sequel to these adventures is recounted in a letter from Freud to Martha.

Woe to you, my Princess, when I come. I will kiss you quite red and feed you till you are plump. And if you are forward you shall see who is the stronger, a gentle little girl who doesn't eat enough or a big wild man who has cocaine in his body. In my last severe depression I took coca again and a small dose lifted me to the heights in a wonderful fashion. I am just now busy collecting the literature for a song of praise to this magical substance.

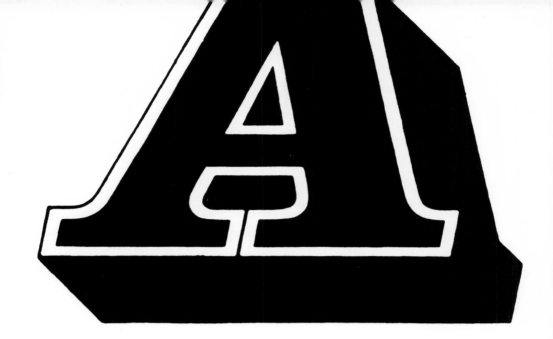

ARCHETYPE

Archetypal enjoyed a "highbrow" popularity, ca. 1946-55; nor is it unknown today.

—Eric Partridge, *Usage and Abusage*

E. S. Carpenter, the anthropologist, wrote about the inability of Robert Graves to grasp the multi-leveled structures. The conventional literary mind naturally tries to "connect" and to classify mythic and symbolic materials by reduction of oral to visual forms of order. Carpenter takes Graves merely as typical of the literary approach to all nonliterate culture. What Carpenter refers to as "adding omissions" is the habit of the visually oriented person to try to find connections where the nonliterate person seeks to create intervals, gaps, and interfaces:

> Graves, not incidentally, has "corrected" Greek mythology in two volumes, eliminating contradictions, adding omissions, arranging lineally, and generally "straightening out." What I am getting at is that they first turn these myths into what they are not; by arranging symbols they create "content"; then they pigeon-hole these various "contents" and come up with archetypes. None of this interests me save the fact that, like Frye, they direct their attention towards a most important problem and, like a hedgehog, build humourless, water-tight systems (with faithful supporters reading "the Book"), that, instead of answering the problem or even illuminating it, block access to it.

Graeme Wilson, introducing his translation of the poems of Hagiwara Sakutaro, cites from the 1882 Japanese translations of early-nineteenth-century English poems:

The Preface sharply attacked the cramping brevity of traditional forms ("How can a consecutive thought be expressed
in such tight forms?"); . . .

The West was discovering the power of discontinuity just when the
East was taking on the excitement of the novelty of the Western
continuum.

Lauriat Lane, Jr., provides a more conventional version of the
archetypal question:

> "The primordial image or archetype is a figure, whether it
> be daemon, man, or process, that repeats itself in the course
> of history wherever creative fantasy is fully manifested. Essen-
> tially, therefore, it is a mythological figure. If we subject
> these images to a closer investigation, we discover them to be
> the formulated resultants of countless typical experiences of
> our ancestors. They are, as it were, the psychic residua of
> numberless experiences of the same type" (Jung, "On the
> Relation of Analytical Psychology to Poetic Art," London,
> 1928).
>
> The crux of Jung's statement lies in the phrase "psychic re-
> sidua," which seems to imply the presence of inherited charac-
> teristics in the mind. Complete scientific proof of such an
> assumption would be impossible, but it is important to recog-
> nize that just as Jung's psychology is continually on the point
> of becoming philosophy, so this scientific-sounding statement
> of what Jung feels to be true is essentially metaphysical and
> must be judged as such. What is of as much value as Jung's
> definition of the archetype, and much more susceptible to
> investigation, is his distinction between the introvertive and
> the extravertive writer, a distinction central to any discussion
> of the use of literary archetypes by a particular author.
>
> —Lauriat Lane, Jr.

19

It might be asked why the word "archetype" should seem to
relate so exclusively to literature. The same question can be asked
of "cliché": why is it almost exclusively verbal in its association?
When I. A. Richards was lecturing at the University of Wisconsin,
he was accidentally immersed in the very cold waters of Lake

Mendota while canoeing. He was rescued in an unconscious condition still clinging to the thwart of the canoe. The student paper *The Cardinal* in a feature cartoon ran the caption: "Saved by a stock response."

Most of us are saved by stock responses in all the nonverbal situations of our lives. It is necessary to consider the incident of the cliché-archetype theme in its nonverbal forms. Language as gesture and cadence and rhythm, as metaphor and image, evokes innumerable objects and situations which are in themselves nonverbal. The extent to which the nonverbal world is shared by language is obscure but no more so than the effect of human artifacts and technological environments on language. We are taking for granted that there is at all times interplay between these worlds of percept and concept, verbal and nonverbal. Anything that can be observed about the behavior of linguistic cliché or archetype can be found plentifully in the nonlinguistic world.

20

> Those masterful images because complete
> Grew in pure mind, but out of what began?
> A mound of refuse or the sweepings of a street,
> Old kettles, old bottles, and a broken can,
> Old iron, old bones, old rags, that raving slut
> Who keeps the till. Now that my ladder's gone,
> I must lie down where all the ladders start,
> In the foul rag-and-bone shop of the heart.
>
> —W. B. Yeats, "The Circus Animals' Desertion"

The human city in all its complexity of functions is thus "a center of paralysis," a waste land of abandoned images. The clue that Yeats offers to the relation between the verbal and the nonverbal cliché and archetype is, in a word, "complete." The most masterful images, when complete, are tossed aside and the process begins anew. Language is a technology which extends all of the human senses simultaneously. All the other human artifacts are, by comparison, specialist extensions of our physical and mental faculties. Written language at once specializes speech by limiting words to one of the senses. Written speech is an example of such specialism, but the spoken word resonates, involving all the senses.

The ancient saying, "Speak that I may see thee," was a popular way of citing this integral and inclusive quality of the spoken word.

If the world of kettles and bottles and broken cans and the world of commerce and money in the till are fragmentary specialisms of man's powers, it becomes easier to see the bond that remains between verbal and nonverbal cliché or archetype. The specialist artifact form has the advantage over language of intensification and amplification far beyond the limits of word or phrase. The archetype is a retrieved awareness or consciousness. It is consequently a retrieved cliché—an old cliché retrieved by a new cliché. Since a cliché is a unit extension of man, an archetype is a quoted extension, medium, technology, or environment.

The following are examples of archetypes which have been chosen to stress the normal tendency of a cliché to cross-quote from one technology to another:

> a flagpole flying a flag
> a cathedral adorned by a stained-glass window
> pipeline carrying oil
> cartoon with a caption
> story with an engraved illustration
> advertisement of a perfume with a sachet of perfume
> electric circuit feeding an electric log fire
> ship with a figurehead
> a mold and its casting

A flagpole flying a flag may become a complex retrieval system. The flag could be the Russian flag, with its hammer and sickle. As flagcloth, the flag could retrieve an entire textile industry. By virtue of the fact that the flag is a national flag, it can retrieve flags of other nations.

The cliché, in other words, is incompatible with other clichés, but the archetype is extremely cohesive; other archetypes' residues adhere to it. When we consciously set out to retrieve one archetype, we unconsciously retrieve others; and this retrieval recurs in infinite regress. In fact, whenever we "quote" one consciousness, we also "quote" the archetypes we exclude; and this quotation of excluded archetypes has been called by Freud, Jung, and others "the archetypal unconscious."

Examples of retrieval systems occur in the Phoenician alphabet, dictionaries, indexes, computers, tables of engineering standards, etc. What these forms retrieve are archetypes or old processes.

It has been observed that civilization has to be recollected by every citizen. Education, whatever guise it takes, is retrieval of the archetype. A dream is a "quoted" experience, that is, it is archetypal—a dream purge rather than a conscious probe.

The common usage of the word "archetype" in literary criticism today has been to consider it more or less under the banner of psychoanalysis. For recent literary criticism it has been a primordial symbol or, as in Yeats, an ancestral symbol. Jung and his disciples have been careful to insist that the archetype is to be distinguished from its expression. Strictly speaking, a Jungian archetype is a power or capacity of the psyche. Nevertheless even in Jung's writings the term is used with interchangeable senses. In *Psyche and Symbol* Jung declares that "the archetype is an element of our psychic structure and thus a vital and necessary component in our psychic economy. It represents or personifies certain instinctive data of the dark primitive psyche; the real, the invisible *roots of consciousness*." Jung is careful to remind literary critics to consider the archetype as a primordial symbol:

> The archetypes are by no means useless archaic survivals or relics. They are living entities, which cause the praeformation of numinous ideas or dominant representations. Insufficient understanding, however, accepts these praeformations in their archaic form, because they have a numinous appeal to the underdeveloped mind. Thus Communism is an archaic, primitive and therefore highly insidious pattern which characterizes primitive social groups. It implies lawless chieftainship as a vitally necessary compensation, a fact which can only be overlooked by means of a rationalistic one-sidedness, the prerogative of the barbarous mind.
>
> It is important to bear in mind that my concept of the "archetypes" has been frequently misunderstood as denoting

inherited patterns of thought or as a kind of philosophical speculation. In reality they belong to the realm of the activities of the instincts and in that sense they represent inherited forms of psychic behaviour. As such they are invested with certain dynamic qualities which, psychologically speaking, are designated as "autonomy" and "numinosity."

Jung accounts for his theory of archetypes by means of the hypothesis of a collective race memory, although he is well aware that there is no scientific acceptance for such an idea. His justification, however, for using the concept of a collective memory is based on the recurrence over a wide area of archetypal patterns in artifacts, literatures, arts, etc., apart from the shaky scientific basis.

José Argüellas, writing on "Compute and Evolve" alludes to the power of the new computer in restoring to contemporary relevance the ancient *I Ching*:

> The I Ching is becoming popular not because it is a refuge from modern life, but because its structure is once again understandable; it is now understandable because men have invented and understand computers—for the way the I Ching works when consulted, with its simple but mathematically flawless system, is much the same way that the computer works. No matter what language system an electronic computer is dependent upon, its functioning is based on the binary system—the same system which, in a simplified way, governs the manipulation of the yarrow stalks or coins which are used in consulting the I Ching. It is not too extravagant to say that, in terms of the nature of the input of the programmerquerent, and of the output, the I Ching can be viewed as a psychic computer. Given the development of computers with all the attendant implications (such as we mentioned earlier on, in referring to ethics), it is not at all odd that many people today are finding the I Ching strangely satisfying. . . .

> The I Ching functions as a computer, and its functioning is only according to the truth of the programming. The truth of the programming depends on how the person who .consults the Book of Changes responds to its messages.

23

AUTHOR AS CLICHÉ (BOOK AS PROBE)

All my poems are on parole.

—Alfeo Marzi

A COAT

I made my song a coat

Covered with embroideries

Out of old mythologies . . .

For there's more enterprise

In walking naked.

—W. B. Yeats

25

Donald M. Frame's biography, *Montaigne*, provides many observations from Montaigne on the transformations in author and in
public that result from a man's image being circulated as a public
probe. The mere amplification-by-repetition that results from the
printed form is a kind of mini-art that causes the author to assume
an iconic mask of corporate dimensions:

If La Boétie had lived, Montaigne would probably have
written in the form of letters:

"Letter writing . . . is a kind of work in which my friends
think I have some ability. And I would have preferred to
adopt this form to publish my sallies, if I had had someone
to talk to. I needed what I once had, a certain relationship to
lead me on, sustain me, and raise me up. . . . I would have
been more attentive and confident, with a strong friend to

address, than I am now, when I consider the various tastes of a whole public. And if I am not mistaken, I would have been more successful."

Elsewhere Montaigne puts the matter in a phrase:

> I owe a complete portrait of myself to the public. The wisdom of my lesson is wholly in truth, in freedom, in reality . . . of which propriety and ceremony are daughters, but bastard daughters. . . . Whoever would wean man of the folly of such a scrupulous verbal superstition would do the world no great harm.

The novelty of self-expression in print seemed to inspire Montaigne with the feeling that he was engaged in a public evacuation or self-degradation. The cathartic aspect of authorship is strongly stressed by Montaigne:

> The sense of the *Essays* as a kind of bottle, or multitude of bottles, in the sea, is clear in the following call from the depths of loneliness:

> "Besides this profit that I derive from writing about myself, I hope for this other advantage, that if my humors happen to please and suit some worthy man before I die, he will try to meet me. I give him a big advantage in ground covered; for all that long acquaintance and familiarity could have gained for him in several years, he can see in three days in this record, and more surely and exactly.
>
> "Amusing notion: many things that I would not want to tell anyone, I *tell the public*; and for my most secret knowledge and thoughts I send my most faithful friends to a bookseller's shop. . . ."

> Montaigne's obscenity continues to grow as a comic reminder of our "peacock's feet."

The comic relation between the book and the members of the body as outerings and utterings of man gets full notice:

> "Each one of my parts," he writes of his penis, "makes me myself just as much as every other one. And no other makes

me more properly a man than this one." Now he offers his
most piquant reminders of the blinkers we wear: "We imagine
much more appropriately an artisan on the toilet seat or on
his wife than a great president, venerable by his demeanor
and his ability." His comments become ever more pungent.
For those who marry their mistresses he quotes the saying:
"Shit in the basket and then put it on your head." About
philosophizers who disdain anything nonintellectual he asks:
"Won't they try to square the circle while perched on their
wives?" His final pages abound in examples; the next-last
paragraph (his last chance for irony before the triumphant
finale) now ends thus: "On the loftiest throne in the world
we are still sitting only on our own rump."

Montaigne took publishing as an innovation that had to be literal.

> As it grows, his obscenity becomes more explicitly didactic.
> To the ancient philosophers, he points out, our notion of
> decency—"not to dare to do openly what it is decent for
> us to do in private"—seemed stupid.

27

W. H. Auden in "In Memory of W. B. Yeats" meditates on the
strange relation between author and public:

> He disappeared in the dead of winter:
> The brooks were frozen, the airports almost deserted, . . .
>
> By mourning tongues
> The death of the poet was kept from his poems.
>
> But for him it was his last afternoon as himself, . . .
> The current of his feeling failed: he became his admirers. . . .
>
> The words of a dead man
> Are modified in the guts of the living.

Baudelaire's line from the envoy to the readers of *Les Fleurs du
Mal*, "*Hypocrite lecteur, mon semblable, mon frère*," encapsulates
all of Auden's thoughts. The reader wears the mask of the poet's
work even as the author puts on the public as a mask. One is probe

for the other. Both are clichés. Joyce put it in a phrase: "My con-sumers, are they not my producers?"

Before print, Thomas à Kempis in his *Imitation of Christ* could venture to offer to the public as a model the Author of our beings. Perhaps all authors have to "play God" in some degree for their public. After all, they *do* make a world. In *The Apes of God* Percy Wyndham Lewis queries the very essence of authors as godlike probes. He portrays them as essentially apes or manipulators of other people's archetypes. Zagreus as super-ape is challenged to produce evidence of what image he is projecting, and the answer seems to be that he is an image of himself as created by the broad-casting medium. The new means of amplifying the dimension of the author's image in the magnetic city tends to project him so naturally into the role of God that the real-life version of this image, whether actor, politician, or artist, is Lilliputian.

CASUISTRY

(ART AS LIE)

Casuistry and the Lie as Derived from Technologies. The Nuncstans of the Written Bond Contrasting with the Gentleman's Word

I always paint fakes.

—Picasso

Tell arts they have no soundness,

But vary by esteeming;

Tell schools they want profoundness,

And stand too much on seeming.

If arts and schools reply,

Give arts and schools the lie.

—Sir Walter Raleigh, "The Lie"

One way of approaching the subject of casuistry is to say that lying becomes easy only when one is dealing through a single medium like print. In dialogue, or interface, lying is much more difficult than in writing, as the legal establishment proclaims. The variety of senses involved in oral discourse, the gestures and tonalities, make lying a kind of dramatic activity, more like making than matching. When "truth" is reduced to mere matching of inner and outer, any statement can be questioned: "Dictionaries drive words out of their senses," as a wag noted.

With the coming of print, the idea of truth as a matching of direct statement against some complex inner state led to the development of a new cult of casuistry and to the whole game of mental reservations. It is explored by Rosalie Colie in *Paradoxia Epidemica*. One of the problems of the multiplicity of printers' Bibles was that many readers could be perturbed by the difficulty of matching the scriptual texts. The harmonizing of the Scriptures became an obsession.

Bacon's essay "Of Truth" opens with allusion to the new games of casuistry that had sprung up with the printed retrieval of whole worlds of conflicting opinions:

> *What is Truth?* said jesting Pilate; and would not stay for an answer. Certainly there be that delight in giddiness, and count it a bondage to fix a belief, affecting free-will in thinking, as well as in acting. And though the sects of philosophers of that kind be gone, yet there remain certain discoursing wits which are of the same veins, though there be not so much blood in them as was in those of the ancients. But it is not only the difficulty and labour which men take in finding out of truth, nor again that when it is found it imposeth upon men's thoughts, that doth bring lies in favour; but a natural though corrupt love of the lie itself. One of the later school of the Grecians examineth the matter, and is at a stand to think what should be in it, that men should love lies, where neither they make for pleasure, as with poets, nor for advantage, as with the merchant, but for the lie's sake. But I cannot tell: this same truth is a naked and open day-light, that doth not shew the masks and mummeries and triumphs of the world half so stately and daintily as candle-lights. Truth may perhaps come to the price of a pearl, that sheweth best by day, but it will not rise to the price of a diamond or carbuncle, that sheweth best in varied lights. The mixture of a lie doth ever add pleasure.

31

In Shakespeare's English histories the form of the trial follows the old medieval procedure of swearing to the probity of an accused person. In later plays such as *Othello* and *Cymbeline*, Shakespeare takes a more modern approach to the credibility of a witness. He is, in a sense, a precursor of the theories of evidence which were developed at the end of the seventeenth century. In both *Othello* and *Cymbeline* the retrieval of "truth" is achieved by the new sensory stress on visual matching that was characteristic of the precision of print itself:

> OTHELLO: . . . Give me the ocular proof;
>   Or by the worth of mine eternal soul
>   Thou hadst been better have been born a dog
>   Than answer my wak'd wrath!
> IAGO: Is't come to this?
> OTHELLO: Make me to see 't; or, at the least, so prove it
>   That the probation bear no hinge nor loop
>   To hang a doubt on; or woe upon thy life!
>
> —*Othello*, Act III, Scene 3

> IACHIMO: If you seek
>   For further satisfying, under her breast—
>   Worthy [the] pressing—lies a mole, right proud
>   Of that most delicate lodging. By my life,
>   I kiss'd it, and it gave me present hunger
>   To feed again, though full. You do remember
>   This stain upon her?
> POSTHUMUS: Ay, and it doth confirm
>   Another stain, as big as hell can hold,
>   Were there no more but it.
>
> —*Cymbeline*, Act II, Scene 5

The popular game of casuistry appears in *Antony and Cleopatra* (Act II, Scene 7):

> MENAS:
>   . . . And, though thou think me poor, I am the man
>   Will give thee all the world.
> POMPEY: Hast thou drunk well?
> MENAS: No, Pompey, I have kept me from the cup.
>   Thou art, if thou dar'st be, the earthly Jove.

> Whate'er the ocean pales, or sky inclips,
> Is thine, if thou wilt ha't.
> POMPEY: Show me which way.
> MENAS: These three world-sharers, these competitors,
>   Are in thy vessel: let me cut the cable;
>   And, when we are put off, fall to their throats.
>   All there is thine.
> POMPEY: Ah, this thou shouldst have done
>   And not have spoken on't! In me 't is villainy;
>   In thee't had been good service. Thou must know,
>   'T is not my profit that does lead mine honour;
>   Mine honour, it. Repent that e'er thy tongue
>   Hath so betray'd thine act. Being done unknown
>   I should have found it afterwards well done
>   But must condemn it now. Desist, and drink.

Ocular proof is dependent on the isolation of one sense as basis for proof. This goes along with Iago as a Machiavellian specialist— divide and rule. Iago is the knowing man who loves fragmentation, breaking people and things up into little bits, which leads to the simple formula "every man has his price."

Ben Franklin in his *Autobiography* presents the same technique of fragmentation as his formula for moral perfection: "I determined to give a week's strict attention to each of the virtues successively." The dehumanizing work by assembly-line repetition and specialism had the great advantage of speed-up. By the same token it eliminated the need for skill or moral quality in hired employees. Gutenberg's assembly-line applied to human expression had many of the advantages and drawbacks.

It is by casuistry that Portia saves Antonio in *The Merchant of Venice*. Dr. Faustus evades the devil by legal chicanery. The precision of print stressed the "loogle leapholes" inherent in the nature of all verbal expression. That is, the new cliché of print retrieved the old archetypes of language as new clichés.

A further evolution of print precision as the father of lies involved the great *Wissenschafters* of the nineteenth century. Richard D. Altick reports "the case of the curious bibliographers."

33

The man that Carter and Pollard were seeking was one extremely well versed in nineteenth-century bibliography. So much was argued by his genius for camouflaging his fake against a background of utterly truthful detail with which only a scholar could have been acquainted. He was equally well versed in the state of the rare-book market; he had a seventh sense that seemed always to tell him what sort of "first edition" would most appeal to the collectors of his day. Finally, he seemed to be in touch with current literary gossip. In selecting works by living authors for his attentions, he was careful to choose the works of those who, for one reason or another, would not be in a position to be asked, or would be temperamentally disinclined to answer, embarrassing questions about these putative first editions. . . .

Carter and Pollard then considered who might have perpetrated this wholesale deception. Years earlier, one or two similar pamphlets had been called into doubt, and suspicion had fallen upon Richard Herne Shepherd and John Camden Hotten, both late Victorian bookmen of qualified integrity. The suspicion rested, it is true, upon the word of only one man, but it was that of a man whose authority in such matters could scarcely be questioned. He was Thomas James Wise, sometime president of the Bibliographical Society, honorary Master of Arts of Oxford, member of the exclusive Roxburghe Club of book collectors, and one of the most learned bibliographers in England. . . . At every turn in their inquiry their clues led them back to the somewhat pontifical gentleman who was the avowed enemy of all sorts of chicanery in bookdealing and -collecting: Thomas James Wise himself.

Today the multimedia have, as noted, demobilized consciousness. We speak of a lie as "credibility gap." "Truth" once again becomes "trust," not Cartesian certainty.

34

CENTENNIAL METAPHOR

Every symbolic system may be a powerful means in organizing affect. This can be proved by the part that symbolic systems as images have played in the history of culture; they are connected with emotions and are widely employed in art, in the theatre, etc., to organize affect.

—A. R. Luriia, *The Nature of Human Conflicts, or Emotion, Conflict and Will*

Many people confuse single objects with symbols. It helps to note the original meaning and structure of the term "symbol" as a juxtaposition of two things. Originally, parties to a contract broke a stick and each took a half. Upon completion of the relationship, the parties juxtaposed the two sticks, creating the *symbol*. It is from *symballein*, Greek for "throwing together."

A kettle is not a symbol unless related or juxtaposed with stove, or pot, or food. Things in isolation are not symbols. Symbolism as an art or technique meant precisely the *breaking* of connections—i.e., syncopation.

The student might easily find himself in a world of chaotic and conflicting suggestions if he were to attempt to use Northrop Frye's definition of a symbol as an exploratory probe:

> SYMBOL: Any unit of any work of literature which can be isolated for critical attention. In general usage restricted to the smaller units, such as words, phrases, images, etc.

The over-all medieval metaphor of the "Book of Nature" was inseparable from the study of the *sacra pagina*, the sacred page of Scripture. The "Book of Creatures" became the metaphor for the world laid out before Adam in the first garden, since we are told in the Scripture that the work of Adam was the viewing and naming of creatures.

Francis Bacon's Solomon's House and the College of the Six Days' Work continues this metaphor as an organizing pattern for modern science which cued the seventeenth-century shift from the controversies over the reading of the sacred page in favor of study of the Book of Nature once more. The interplay between the two books of Scripture and Nature never had a more vigorous period than the eighteenth and nineteenth centuries. The new techniques of anthropology and biology in the nineteenth century brought the Book of Nature to the Book of Scripture in the name of the higher criticism.

In the seventeenth century, with Bishop Sprat's *History of the Royal Society*, the Book of Nature is equivalent to the Book of Revelation. By the time of the second edition of John Locke's *Essay Concerning Human Understanding*, the Book of Nature has gained a preference because it is thought to be a universal revelation as compared to the arbitrary and particular revelation of Scripture. By the end of the eighteenth century, with deists like Thomas Paine, or, on the other hand, writers like William Blake, the Book of Nature has developed as many difficulties or stumbling blocks as the Book of Revelation.

Newton was in a continuous tradition of interrelating the two Books of Nature and of Scripture when he devoted a large part of his life to his commentary on the Book of Daniel. In the early part of the seventeenth century the Book of Nature as an alternate expression of the Book of Creatures and "Nature" usually means animal or human natures, rather than simply external Nature. Thomas Browne joined the two books in his famous phrase about "man, the great amphibian, living in divided and distinguished worlds." Even before Sir Thomas Browne, Descartes had explained that the animals were essentially animal machines. With Descartes, both the page of Nature and the page of Scripture had been desacralized.

In Pope's *Essay on Man*, the Book of Nature has been converted into a "chain of beings," and in the nineteenth century the first man receives the dubious distinction of being "the missing link" in

37

this chain. The notable ambiguity of the *Essay* is the alternative reading: "A mighty maze! and all without a plan," or "A mighty maze! but not without a plan."

Both the page of Scripture and that of Nature had been comforting truths until the nineteenth century. When the journalistic principle of bad news came into vogue, both Scripture and Nature became fruitful sources of painful truths. The nineteenth century produced many uniform metaphors applicable to the entire human situation, e.g., those of Darwin, Herbert Spencer, Comte, Marx, Jung, Freud, and Frazer.

Just when the circulating libraries were disillusioning Samuel Taylor Coleridge with the world of the novel, and distressing him with the spectacle of the corruption of taste and morals through this kind of entertainment, the newspaper was coming in as the new technological cliché. Lamartine, in 1830, said, "The book arrives too late." The daily newspaper he saw as a new technology, creating a liaison between the public and the writer every twenty-four hours, whereas the book took weeks and months to establish the same relation. The speed with which the printed word now related public and the author turned the author into a corporate one, and this distressed people like John Stuart Mill, Carlyle, and Matthew Arnold, who saw the new situation as tragic. But just when the press had established this new cliché form of corporate perception, the probing scholars were already reaching back to retrieve a mythic, and corporate, tribal past through archaeology and anthropology.

Just as the book was losing its power to create high culture in the individual reader, the press seemed to spur the strivings to recover the human corporate, tribal past. So, with the disappearance of the book as cliché, or perceptual probe, and the arrival of the corporate press, there also returns the possibility of new acquaintance with and mastery of myth. Ritual returned as a means of organizing for poetry and the arts. This new resource appears in the work of Wagner. Byron and Browning actually attempted newspaper epics in *Don Juan* and *The Ring and the Book*. Mallarmé followed, and the newspaper epic was fully realized in James Joyce's *Ulysses*.

The development of print technologies provided the matrix for all the mass-production techniques of the industrial age. The seventeenth century was an age when people were trying out all sorts of new techniques—the building of bridges, the building of dams, and new kinds of agricultural machinery. With this general interest in mechanical invention comes the use of the metaphor of the machine. The clock cliché, even more than the *camera oscura* or the perspective of glass, is perhaps the most famous of these mechanical metaphors. Naturally the clock metaphor presupposed the image of the cycloidal jaws of the suspended pendulum. Pope, in his *Essay on Man*, doesn't refer to the Book of Nature as a volume of creatures. He thinks of it as a chain of being.

Sterne in *Tristram Shandy* is a comic artist dealing with the problems of mechanism and the fascination for the machine analogy of his contemporaries, and he rather enjoys pointing out to them the flaws in the machine. He sees the machine as running down, wearing out. Later on, the evolutionists, when they take over the volume of creatures as chain of being, pitch upon the weak point, which is "the missing link." It becomes the next cliché technology for apprehending nature.

Symbolism is the art of the missing link, as the word implies: *sym-ballein*, to throw together. It is the art of syncopation. It is the basis of electricity and quantum mechanics, as Lewis Carroll understood via Lobachevski, and non-Euclidean geometries. The chemical bond, as understood by Heisenberg and Linus Pauling, is RESONANCE. Echoland. The world of acoustic space whose center is everywhere and whose margin is nowhere, like the pun.

Art and Nature alike begin to involve the entire public, whether via jazz or the mystery story. The centralizing imagery of the zeitgeisters and the transcendentalists is sloughed off as old Euclidean cliché. The new age of discontinuity retrieves all the cultures at once. Everyman becomes a missing link? A hairless ape?

The function of temporal cliché is to select for use one item or one feature out of a vast middenheap of mythological materials. It may be that the cue for selection occurs when, from the rationale of a dominant cliché complex, we make a deprecatory adjustment toward the unconscious or the irrational, suppressed by the action of that cliché—e.g., *Gesundheit!* The function of a temporal cliché depends upon the suppression of huge quantities of unconscious archetypal materials. In the same way a news "story" exists consciously by the suppression of nearly all the materials available.

A mind has many rationales; a cliché probe stresses only one of these at a time. The others are dismissed into the unconscious. "Superstitions" can be regarded as absurdist recognitions of alternative rationales—e.g., the inner trip as new centennial metaphor.

The "great chain of being" that had served as a metaphor for the eighteenth century, whether in Lockean chains of association or in the chain-stitch of the later sewing machines, carried over incongruously into the nineteenth-century revolutionary hypothesis of the "missing link." Just as NASA scientists are still locked up in the world of Newtonian visual space, so physicists are still loyal to the stop-response of literary mechanism when they speak of "chain reactions."

The new cult of ESP is a natural adjunct to telecommunications. When you put your nervous system outside as a world environment, ESP would seem to be rather "Plurabelle." Edward T. Hall's *The Silent Language* stresses the new awareness of languages as structures of awareness and patterns of gesture:

> The can-may distinction illustrates one of the many different types of informal patterns that exist in our language. Another type is associated with the use of what is technically known as the *superfix* first identified by Trager. The reader is familiar with prefixes and suffixes that are added at the beginnings and ends of stems. The superfix, as the word implies, goes over or above the utterance.
>
> By identifying the superfix Trager raised a whole category of grammatical and other events from the informal to the technical. That ill-defined, highly significant agglomeration of vocalizations known as "tone of voice" began to be unraveled by identification of the superfix. The difference between an adjectival and a nominal is signaled by the use of superfixes, in this case varying degrees of loudness or stress. For example, in English the difference in the spoken language between green house (the color green), greenhouse (where

plants are grown), and the Green house (house owned by Mr. and Mrs. Green) is solely a function of varying stress. The French, incidentally, do not share this pattern with us and cannot hear the difference between these three utterances. The new rules of grammar for English, when they eventually appear, may describe adjectivals in terms of their stress pattern in relation to other items.

CLICHÉ/ARCHETYPE

AS SYSTOLE-DIASTOLE

Whereas Bergson says robotized behavior is the source of civilized laughter, Wyndham Lewis says non-robotized behavior is the mirth of the wild body.

> . . . there will be time
> To prepare a face to meet the faces that you meet;
> There will be time to murder and create,
> And time for all the works and days of hands . . .
>
> —T. S. Eliot, "The Love Song of J. Alfred Prufrock"

Eliot refers to the *Works and Days* of Hesoid, the ritual hymn of what Eliade calls "the regeneration of the world and life through repetition of the cosmogony" (The Myth of the Perpetual Return). Eliot's work is often devoted to showing the translation of this rhythm of creation and destruction into the merely industrial form of fragmented mass production. This latter form alienates man rather than involves man. The moment of truth created by the artist permits the return of the dead:

> The creation of the world, then, is reproduced every year. Allah is he who effects the creation, hence he repeats it (*Qur'ân*, X, 4 f.). This eternal repetition of the cosmogonic act, by transforming every New Year into the inauguration of an era, permits the return of the dead to life, and maintains the hope of the faithful in the resurrection of the body. We shall soon return to the relations between the New Year ceremonies and the cult of the dead. At this point let us note that the beliefs, held almost everywhere, according to which the dead return to their families (and often return as "living dead") at the New Year season (during the twelve days between Christmas and Epiphany) signify the hope that the abolition of time is possible at this mythical moment, in which the world is destroyed and re-created. The dead can come

back now, for all barriers between the dead and the living are broken (is not primordial chaos reactualized?), and they will come back because at this paradoxical instant time will be suspended, hence they can again be contemporaries of the living. Moreover, since a new Creation is then in preparation, they can hope for a return to life that will be enduring and concrete.

—Mircea Eliade, *Cosmos and History*

Hans Selye in *From Dream to Discovery* illustrates how the act of discovery tends to occur just at the moment of going to sleep or just at the moment of awakening, that is, between two states:

As I have said repeatedly, intuitive ideas commonly present themselves on the fringe of consciousness, while falling asleep or awakening. Therefore, I like to go over my problem just before retiring—or even in the middle of the night if I happen to wake up—always keeping pencil and paper within reach even at night because nocturnal ideas tend to vanish, leaving no trace by the morning.

44

Milton shows the very same dual process which Eliot cites in "to murder and create" where he describes the insurrection of Satan:

Before thir eyes in sudden view appear
The secrets of the hoarie deep, a dark
Illimitable Ocean without bound,
Without dimension, where length, breadth, and highth,
And time and place are lost; where eldest Night
And *Chaos*, Ancestors of Nature, hold
Eternal *Anarchie*, amidst the noise
Of endless warrs, and by confusion stand.

—John Milton, *Paradise Lost*, Book II

Satan's cliché thrust fails, landing him in Chaos. Milton couldn't have provided a better paradigm of the ambitious probe situation. A parallel occurs in *Macbeth*:

MACBETH: If it were done when 'tis done, then 'twere well
    It were done quickly. If the assassination

Could trammel up the consequence, and catch
With his surcease success; that but this blow
Might be the be-all and the end-all here,
But here, upon this bank and [shoal] of time,
We'd jump the life to come. But in these cases
We still have judgement here, that we but teach
Bloody instructions, which, being taught, return
To plague th' inventor. This even-handed justice
Commends th' ingredients of our poison'd chalice
To our own lips. He's here in double trust:
First, as I am his kinsman and his subject,
Strong both against the deed; then, as his host,
Who should against his murderer shut the door,
Not bear the knife myself.

—*Macbeth*, Act V, Scene 7

Macbeth thinks in terms of the cliché-technologies of the knife and trammel net as means of murdering and creating, of probing and retrieving. His knife will destroy Duncan, that is, monarchy itself. "We will proceed no further in this business." The cliché of the knife as an instrument of ambition will destroy monarchy and order and all the political clichés of society. By scrapping all order, he will set up a school in which all will learn "bloody instructions." There will be nothing left to retrieve but the scrapped clichés of violence. Joyce capsulated this moment of Macbeth's vision in his phrase: "A burning would is come to dance inane. Glamours hath moidered's lieb . . ."

The very techniques by which one achieves desirable innovations, destroy most of the pre-existing achievements and require a new creation. The "tragic flaw" is not a detail of characterization, a mere "fly in the ointment," but a structural feature of ordinary consciousness.

A far more tragic instance of Macbeth's dilemma is described by Anatol Rappoport in his Introduction to *Clausewitz on War*:

The experience of the Second World War was an exhilarating one for Americans because of the dramatic sequence of events: initial defeats, followed by a turning of the tide and rapidly accumulating victories. War became fixed in the

45

American imagination as an extreme effort which one undertakes only when provoked, hence only when one is in the right.
Such an effort, to Americans' way of thinking, was bound to
be victorious. In other words, identification with the protagonists of good (as in mass-entertainment dramas) and a
confident expectation of victory became the context in which
the majority of Americans thought about war.

The basic reason for this dilemma of cliché innovation as involving "massive retaliations" (which Macbeth had hoped to
"trammel up") is "the common appetites of the business and
military machines. Both thrive on unlimited growth. The two
Establishments nurture each other."

Arthur Koestler in *The Act of Creation* observes the same
"dialogue" or systole-diastole movement in another field:

Thus, contrary to appearances and beliefs, science, like
poetry or architecture or painting, has its genres, "movements," schools, theories which it pursues with increasing
perfection until the level of saturation is reached where all is
done and said—and then embarks on a new approach, based
on a different type of curiosity, a different scale of values. . . .

The same movement is found in the age-old theme of ends and
means. New cliché, new technology retrieves unexpected archetypes from the rag-and-bone shop. New means create new ends
as new services create new discomforts. New speed-up, a new
rim-spin put around any slower organization, destroys the slower
one.

Overkill, the technologies for total destruction of mankind and
the planet, create a "peace" that passeth all technology. Bernard
Mandeville built his *Fable of the Bees* on the same observation:
"Private vices, public benefits."

Machiavelli saw the new private morality created by the new
specialist technology of print as creating new political goals. The
theme echoes through all the situations of the culture: "When
success a lover's toil attends, few ask if fraud or force attend his
end."

CLICHÉ
AS
BREAKDOWN

You've tasted your worm

You've hissed my mystery lectures

You will leave by the next town drain.

> —Don to delinquent undergraduates

You can't beat English lawns. Our final hope

Is flat despair.

> —William Empson, "Rolling the Lawn"

48   Sliding down the razor-blade of life.

> —Tom Lehrer

The way to make a film is to begin with

an earthquake and work up to a climax.

> —C. B. De Mille

One of the richest insights into the state of English appeared in *Harper's Magazine* in 1915 when William Dean Howells wrote: "With us Americans the popular taste is so bad, so ignorant, so vulgar, that it suggests the painful doubt whether literacy is a true test of intelligence and a rightful proof of citizenship. . . . The literary taste of the Russian Jews on the East Side is superior to that of the average native American." The average adult male Jew, Leo Rosten points out, has always been accustomed to handling at least three languages. The intervals, or breaks, between these three or more languages have constituted a perpetual interface and inspiration to Jewish communities. Their homelessness has been a major cultural asset.

All hardware "growth" is destruction. It is merely additive, as in cities or industries.

ONE BIG CITY IS ONLY ROUTE
TO EFFICIENCY OFFICIALS CLAIM
—*Toronto Daily Star*, March 26, 1969

The celebrated documentary *A Place to Stand*, done for Expo 1967 by Christopher Chapman, celebrates the growth of Ontario by a terrifying series of images of destruction. It is a drama of strip-mining of natural resources and the crunching of old motor cars into little cubic capsules—all done in raving color.

The famous *Potemkin* of Eisenstein is not an involuntary critique of a regime, like a Chaplin film, but a deliberate satire. Elémire Zolla's comment on *Potemkin* draws attention to the hilarious technique of juxtaposing a dilapidated baby carriage with the vast expanse of palace steps:

> Must criticism of the Tsarist regime, in order to persuade those unable to judge in any other manner, depend on the baby carriage in the movie *Potemkin* bumping down a stairway in Odessa? For one aware of the symbols offered by history, not the "significant and moving details" (the journalistic stereotypes that aptly describe the cinematic vision of reality), dwelling on that baby carriage is a doltish self-indulgence, like the man who enjoys using debased words, dialect curses, and brothel obscenities to give force to a political judgment.

Zolla continues with a pathetic fallacy of misplaced concreteness that exceeds Joyce himself:

> Of course the baby carriage in Odessa is not in itself abject. It is only elementary, not very rigorous, loaded at once with concrete clarity and sentimental mawkishness—a sentimen-

49

tality and colorless objectivity alien to each other and yet coexistent, presented in a covert, fraudulent manner, since the cinematic sequence seems to confuse and merge them.

Ovid's *Metamorphoses* follow the complementarity of Hertz's dictum, "The consequences of the images are the images of the consequences," illustrating "all growth as destruction," as both "murdering and creating." The technique of metamorphosis as a chemical change is by interface of two elements, or two situations. Thus in all metamorphic literature there is a plot and a subplot, e.g., Shakespeare's *Venus and Adonis,* with its two pursuits: Venus pursues Adonis, and Adonis pursues the boar. She bores him silly, and the beast bores him to death. Following a great deal of dumb play, "once more the engine of her thoughts began."

Shakespeare smashes all the old clichés of love up to his time and concludes with a curse on love. This doubleness persists through all of Shakespeare's sonnets and tragedies. Can any art exist without it? The movie, as a "reel world," at once sets up an interface with the real.

The Waste Land opens with a drum-roll of clichés, which characterizes all of Eliot's work. With the hula hoop, children abandoned the lineal rolling operation in favor of dancing and involvement. The clash between the old and the new use of the hoop heralded a complete change in cultural mores from the mechanical to the electrical. When the bicycle ceases to be a vehicle, it becomes a toy, witness the new Mustang bikes as perfect example of "pastimes are past times."

Karl Polanyi's *The Great Transformation* is the story of the shift from private to corporate awareness in nineteenth-century society and politics. The couplet form which ruled English poetry for centuries inevitably uses the double plot in capsule:

> The hungry judges soon the sentence sign,
> and wretches hang that jurymen may dine.

This is a kind of haiku which reveals the monstrosities, or the miscarriages, of justice. The judges are not hungry for justice. They appear as cannibals, as much as the jurymen themselves. Any cliché, pushed to a high degree, is scrapped in favor of a new cliché which may be the revival of an old one—e.g., old cliché as new archetype = old archetype as new cliché.

A connoisseur of the seventeenth-century double-plot, William Empson, observes apropos its logical economy: "*therefore* is a punch on the nose."

CLICHÉ AS PROBE

Slander, let it lie its flattest, has never been able to convict our good and great and no ordinary Southron Earwicker, that homogenius man, as a pious author called him . . .

—James Joyce, *Finnegans Wake*

Thus his personality as a mass-man is reflected: at once boundlessly presumptuous and modest to the point of self-annihilation. He says, if he wishes to damn a given work, "I don't understand it"; and this is his formula for the most severe condemnation, for if *his* comprehension cannot encompass it, how can anyone dare to affirm that the work is comprehensible? And then he adds: "But I don't really know much about it."

—Elémire Zolla, *The Eclipse of the Intellectual*

The extreme usefulness of cliché to all students is illustrated in the following passage:

> What, therefore, is a cliché? Perhaps intellectual and intelligent opinion has not yet been so far crystallized as to justify a definition. *The Oxford English Dictionary* says that it is a "stereotyped expression, a commonplace phrase." I should (*ex cathedra ignorantiae*, as Mr. Humbert Wolfe once said wittily of someone else) like to enlarge on that definition and render it more practical, more comprehensive. The origin of the term may help, for, as Littré shows, *cliché* is the sub-

stantivized participle of *clicher*, a variant of *cliquer*, "to click"; *clicher* is a die-sinkers' term for "to strike melted lead in order to obtain a cast"; hence, a cliché is a stereotyped expression—a phrase "on tap" as it were—and this derivative sense, which has been current in France since the early 'eighties, came to England ca. 1890. *Revenons à nos moutons* (cliché). A cliché is an outworn commonplace; a phrase, or short sentence, that has become so hackneyed that careful speakers and scrupulous writers shrink from it because they feel that its use is an insult to the intelligence of their audience or public: "a coin so battered by use as to be defaced" (George Baker). Clichés range from fly-blown phrases ("much of a muchness"; "to all intents and purposes"), metaphors that are now pointless ("lock, stock and barrel"), formulas that have become mere counters ("far be it from me to . . .")—through sobriquets that have lost all their freshness and most of their significance ("the Iron Duke")—to quotations that are nauseating ("cups that cheer but not inebriate"), and foreign phrases that are tags ("longo intervallo", "bête noire").

—Eric Partridge, *A Dictionary of Clichés*

A teacher asked her class to use a familiar word in a new way. One boy read: "The boy returned home with a cliché on his face." Asked to explain his phrase, he said, "The dictionary defines *cliché* as a "worn-out expression."

The notion that our perceptions themselves are clichés patterned by the many hidden environmental structures of culture has been extensively explored in our time. The studies extend from *The Silent Language* of Edward T. Hall to *Patterns of Culture* by Ruth Benedict, *The Structure or Scientific Revolutions* by Thomas Kuhn, *Remembering* by F. C. Bartlett, *Emotion* by James Hillman, and *Propaganda* by Jacques Ellul.

For example, Hillman remarks, "Not only does a perception release latent energy, but it also can cause the formation of new, tense psychical systems which—as with Kafka—are the basis of emotion." What is common to all these approaches is the awareness that cliché is not necessarily verbal, and that it is also an active, structuring, probing feature of our awareness. It performs multiple functions from release of emotion to retrieval of other clichés from both the conscious and unconscious life. The very term "cliché" derives from printing—the die-maker's great contribution to language. Print was, before the electric age, the principal cliché means of retrieving the past.

The banishing of the cliché from serious attention was the natural gesture of literary specialists. The Theater of the Absurd has shown us some of the creative contemporary uses of cliché. Nothing could be more banal than an old coat or a coat-hanger. Yeats created one of his most memorable visions by means of these properties:

> Because there is safety in derision
> I talked about an apparition,
> I took no trouble to convince,
> Or seem plausible to a man of sense,
> Distrustful of that popular eye
> Whether it be bold or sly.
> *Fifteen apparitions have I seen;*
> *The worst a coat upon a coat-hanger.*
>
> —W. B. Yeats, "The Apparitions"

55

The writers of composition texts have made much of the cliché as they understand it. They are right in saying that the cliché ought to get great critical attention. Its real significance lies in the fact that all access to consciousness is tentative and uncertain. The simplest definition of cliché is a "probe" (in any of the multitudinous areas of human awareness) which promises information but very often provides mere retrieval of old clichés. The starting point of this book, then, is the "green-as-grass," "quick-as-a-fox," "brown-as-a-berry," "as-right-as-rain" cliché. The resemblances between this sort of cliché and the auto engine as cliché are spectacular.

Language is, of course, man's greatest and most complex artifact, every word of which extends or involves all of his sensory life.

His other technologies are, in comparison, very specialized and fragmentary. Even pets—"Love me, love my dog," or "Love thy label as thyself"—indicate sensory extensions of deep human significance even when they have lost their functional survival value.

Logan Pearsall Smith in *Words and Idioms* lists famous idioms derived from the use of dogs in hunting and the chase. In principle, these illustrate the genetic origins of all clichés:

To bristle up,
To set by the ears (?),
To fly in the face of,
To turn tail,
To go off with one's tail between one's legs,
A dog in the manger,
A lucky dog,
A sly dog,
A hang-dog look,
Top dog,
Under dog,

Any stick good enough to beat a dog with,
Love me, love my dog,
Every dog has its day,
Scornful dogs will eat dirty puddings,
A bone of contention,
His bark is worse than his bite,
Too old to learn new tricks,
Not to have a word to throw to a dog.

To "stave off" comes from bear-baiting. The dog generates these clichés: through the dog man escapes from goal-seeking.

To come to heel,
To hold in leash,
To slip the collar,
To give the slip to,
To hound on,
To hit it off [the scent],
To hunt down,
To have a good, or bad, nose for,
To run to earth,
To run with the hare and hunt with the hounds,

To throw to the pack,
To throw off the scent,
To make a dead set at,
To be on the track of (?),
To keep, or lose, track of (?),
To cover one's tracks (?),
In full cry,
In at the death,
A red herring,
Hue and cry.

These verbal residues from man's primordial technologies illustrate the way in which cliché develops. Any extension of man's sensory life such as the dog, or the motor car, imprints numerous clichés on any language, extending its range of probe.

All media of communications are clichés serving to enlarge man's scope of action, his patterns of association and awareness. These media create environments that numb our powers of attention by sheer pervasiveness. The limits of our awareness of these forms does not limit their action upon our sensibilities. Just as the rim-spin of the planet arranges the components of high- and low-pressure areas, so the environments created by linguistic and other extensions of our powers are constantly creating new climates of thought and feeling. Since the resulting symbolic systems are numerous, they are in perpetual interplay, creating a kind of sound-light show on an ever-increasing scale.

These hidden symbolic systems are completely phony, or resonating pseudo-events of our own manufacture, since they stem from man's own psyche. This view is memorably expressed by George Orwell in *1984.* Syme, speaking of the language of the future, contrasts its aims: "Don't you see that the whole aim of Newspeak is to narrow the range of thought? In the end we shall make thoughtcrime literally impossible, because there will be no words in which to express it. Every concept that can ever be needed will be expressed by exactly *one* word, with its meaning rigidly defined and all its subsidiary meanings rubbed out and forgotten. Already . . . we're not far from that point. . . . Every year fewer and fewer words, and the range of consciousness always a little smaller. . . ." Some might ask, what is the difference between the "purification" of language urged by scientific method and the "destruction of words" described by Orwell.

Orwell speaks for the literati, for whom all nonverbal modes of consciousness are questionable.

Shakespeare enjoyed the slang clichés of his time as much as Ionesco:

> HAMLET: It shall to the barber's, with your beard. Prithee, say on; he's for a jig or a tale of bawdry, or he sleeps. Say on; come to Hecuba.
>
> FIRST PLAYER: "But who, O, who had seen the [mobled] queen"—

HAMLET: "The 'mobled' queen"?
POLONIUS: That's good; " 'mobled' queen" is good.

—Hamlet, Act II, Scene 2

Polonius hit upon the "crunch" epithet of the play. Hamlet is "hung up" (old twentieth-century slang) on Hecuba:

What's Hecuba to him, or he to Hecuba,
That he should weep for her? What would he do,
Had he the motive and the cue for passion
That I have? He would drown the stage with tears
And cleave the general ear with horrid speech,
Make mad the guilty and appall the free,
Confound the ignorant, and amaze indeed
The very faculty of eyes and ears.
Yet I,
A dull and muddy-mettled rascal, peak
Like John-a-dreams, unpregnant of my cause,
And can say nothing; no, not for a king.

—Hamlet, Act II, Scene 3

58

Paradoxically, Hamlet accuses himself of being numbed and stupefied. It is the very cliché, or stereotype qualifying of the actor's performance, that awakens him. Such can be the function of cliché at any time for anybody. Initially any cliché is a breakthrough into a new dimension of experience. Alfred North Whitehead mentions in *Science and the Modern World* that the great discovery of the nineteenth century was the discovery of the technique of discovery. The art of discovery itself is now a cliché, and creativity has become a stereotype of the twentieth century. In the *Discourse on Method* Descartes considers the art of discovery against a background of scrapped syllogism. He finds that the readier way to solve a problem is to break it down into its various parts and to keep running over these again and again in his mind until he "intuits" a solution—that is, until a breakthrough occurs.

Another approach to cliché is to point out that the more deeply people participate in a culture, the less the motive for innovation. (This question is examined further in the Eye-Ear section.) May it not be, however, that the staying-power of clichés, like that of old songs and nursery rhymes, derives from the involvement they demand? Literary culture, by definition, is highly visual and detached and breeds a great craving for innovation as a means of vitality. The technical bias of any culture is revealed where there is the greatest multiplicity of terms for the same operations—for instance, the Eskimo has many words for "snow." The Americans have many words for cars and dances. Now the superflux of new dance forms has ended the naming of dances altogether. In *The Book of Tea* we are told that the function of art is to accommodate man to the changing present. In a world of endless innovation, art never had so much to do as in the past century. "Make it new" is a mere necessity of art today. It is the newness that produces the clichés, or probes. These, as with Hamlet and the Theater of the Absurd, provide a sting of perception and the shock of recognition.

The *nuncstans* constitute an eternal present of clichés which, like the stereotypes on the Grecian urn, "do tease us out of thought." Marlowe in *Dr. Faustus* achieves the sense of the eternal "now" of the cliché probe by continually reiterating in an emphatic position the adverb "now."

A contradiction arises in literate cultures from the fact of the printed form as a snapshot of mental processes. The revolution against the limitations of this stasis became universal in the nineteenth century, in its concern with art as process. Pater immortalized this new obsession in his injunction to "burn always with a hard gemlike flame." His star pupil, Gerard Manley Hopkins, reveals the technical source of this aesthetic cliché in his great lines: "The fine delight that fathers thought; the strong spur, live and lancing like the blowpipe flame, . . ." Hopkins merges the aggressive Bengal Lancer with the blowtorch.

Hopkins, in this allusion, anticipates the great flood of technological clichés that poured from Rudyard Kipling (better known to the leftist decades as "mudguard dripping"). The same concern extends to all fields of biology, psychology, and learning.

However, the roots of Western literate culture, beginning with Plato, are in the discovery of the "eternal forms" as an ideal norm. With Plato and the onset of the Euclidean age arose the desire for absolute fixity of geometric form in art and architecture. The sudden shift of attention to process, as in Machiavelli, seemed then a betrayal of our culture. This shift in emphasis as analyzed by Descartes, Newton, Blake, and Darwin was to be called "the creative imagination" by the Romantics. In the seventeenth-century theater, Iago, an opportunist and an artist who shaped lives by his power, presents the creative principle within process. Shakespeare finds it necessary to mask Iago with a diabolic surface. In Shakespeare's sonnets the theme of the close union of creativity and destructivity becomes a crux, the master-mistress (miss-stress).

One of the richest areas of the probing cliché is in the world of legal terminology and procedure. "Snooping with intent to creep" is still an indictable offense. F. W. Maitland's *The Forms of Action at Common Law* explores a whole world of legal cliché as complex probes and controls in social action. In common law, or oral tradition, the great complexity and rigidity of structures produced the commonplace: where there is no remedy there is no wrong.

> The key-note of the form of action is struck by the original writ, the writ whereby the action is begun. From of old the rule has been that no one can bring an action in the king's courts of common law without the king's writ; we find this rule in Bracton—*Non potest quis sine brevi agere.* That rule we may indeed say has not been abolished even in our own day. The first step which a plaintiff has to take when he brings an action in the High Court of Justice is to obtain a writ. But there has been a very great change.

In the eleventh and twelfth centuries, with the rise of writs, all tended toward homogeneity and centralism. Just as Henry Maine's classic *From Status to Contract* follows the process of social change initiated by written forms, so Maitland shows how large sovereign or nationalist states arose via the same agency of the writ (and the speedy courier system that goes with a paper-based bureaucracy):

> But now, when the forms of action are gone, when we are no longer under any temptation to make them more rational than they were, the truth might be discovered and be told, and one part of the truth is assuredly this, that throughout

the early history of the forms of action there is an element of struggle, of struggle for jurisdiction. In order to understand them we must not presuppose a centralized system of justice, an omni-competent royal or national tribunal; . . .

The old clichés of oral evidence came into stark conflict with the new writs of the eleventh century (under William the Conqueror) and of the twelfth century. The great disaster date of British history is not 1066 but 1086, the year of The Domesday Book.

Many landholders were dispossessed by the sudden demand to "prove" their rights. The demand was for documentary evidence of ownership dating back to the days of Edward the Confessor. A more vivid example of legal clichés scrapping current clichés and reviving ancient clichés or archetypes would be hard to find. It all worked to the benefit of the centralizing royal power. Scholars since Maitland have discovered that whereas individual landowners were unable to produce documentary evidence of their rights, the monasteries, because of their great temporal stability and scribal resources, were able to forge ample documentary proof of their ancient and prescriptive rights to their holdings. There grew up swarms of forgers, like Chaucer's Man of Law, who could produce "genuine fakes" as rapidly as anybody in more enlightened times.

As an example of how legal cliché can inspire great drama, Maitland notes: "In the reign of Henry III Bracton had said . . . 'There may be as many forms of action as there are causes of action.' " This suggests, truly enough for us, that in order of logic, Right comes before Remedy. "There ought to be a remedy for every wrong" is a reversal of the oral code's recognition of "Where there is no remedy there is no wrong." That is, with the rise of the written law, matching takes over from making. The punishment must *fit* the crime. There must be punishment, even if there is no remedy. In our own time, judges, when they hand down suspended sentences, recognize prisons as infallible receipts for making criminals.

CONSCIOUSNESS

What I call the "auditory imagination" is the feeling for syllable and rhythm, penetrating far below the conscious levels of thought and feeling, invigorating every word; sinking to the most primitive and forgotten, returning to the origin and bringing something back, seeking the beginning and the end. It works through meanings, certainly, or not without meanings in the ordinary sense, and fuses the old and obliterated and the trite, the current, and the new and surprising, the most ancient and the most civilized mentality.

—T. S. Eliot

63

In archaic societies, "the people of the dream," the conscious life is flooded with the images of what civilized man thrusts back into the unconscious. Individual consciousness is achieved by strategic ignorance and suppression. Man's right to his own ignorance might be said to be his principal means of private identity. One of the techniques of the poet and the artist, it has been pointed out, is to contrive situations that will dislocate the mind into awareness. The unconscious could be called the "scrubbing" of the present, just as printing and other technologies are means for retrieving the past.

Yeats's "Byzantium" begins:

> The unpurged images of day recede;
> The Emperor's drunken soldiery are abed;
> Night resonance recedes, night-walker's song
> After great cathedral gong; . . .

Yeats assumes that sleep is a process of purging the images of the day by a *ricorso*, or rehearsal, such as constitutes the entire action of *Finnegans Wake*:

> . . . wiped all his sinses, martial and menial . . . excremuncted as freely as any frothblower.

Reading at an ordinary speed of a few hundred words per minute pushes most of a book into the unconscious, whereas speed-reading at several thousand words a minute, by highlighting the dance of meaning at the expense of word and syntax, is a Theater of the Absurd, since it confronts the reader with the clichés of thought. Joyce is everywhere comically aware of this:

> Yet to concentrate solely on the literal sense or even the psychological content of any document to the sore neglect of the enveloping facts themselves circumstantiating it is just as hurtful to sound sense (and let it be added to the truest taste) as were some fellow . . . straightway to run off and vision her plump and plain in her natural altogether, preferring to close his blinkhard's eyes to the ethiquethical fact that she was, after all, wearing for the space of the time being some definite articles of evolutionary clothing . . .

The city as a means of heightening human consciousness by stepping up the intensity of human interface receives eerie treatment from Norman Mailer in *Miami and the Siege of Chicago*:

> . . . the famous stockyards of Chicago were at night as empty as the railroad sidings of the moon. Long before the Democratic Convention of 1968 came to the Chicago Amphitheatre, indeed eighteen years ago when the reporter had paid his only previous visit, the area was even then deserted at night, empty as the mudholes on a battlefield after a war has passed. West of the Amphitheatre, railroad sidings seem to continue on for miles, accompanied by those same massive low sheds larger than armories, with pens for tens of thousands of frantic beasts, cattle, sheep and pigs, animals in an orgy of gorging and dropping and waiting and smelling blood. . . .
>
> The animals passed a psychic current back along the over-

head trolley—each cut throat released its scream of death into the throat not yet cut and just behind, and that penultimate throat would push the voltage up, drive the current back and further back into the screams of every animal upside down and hanging from that clanking overhead trolley, bare electric bulbs screaming into the animal eye and brain, gurglings and awesome hollows of sound coming back from the open plumbing ahead of the cut jugular as if death were indeed a rapids along some underground river, and the fear and absolute anguish of beasts dying upside down further ahead passed back along the line, back all the way to the corrals and the pens, back even to the siding with the animals still in boxcars, back, who knew—so high might be the psychic voltage of the beast —back to the farm where first they were pushed into the truck which would take them to the train. . . .

Well, the smell of the entrails and that agonized blood electrified by all the outer neons of ultimate fear got right into the grit of the stockyard stench.

65

Mailer concentrates on the osmic space of the great "hog-butcher of the world." The city as a vast waste land, junkyard, or museum of artifacts is the theme of all the epics from the *Iliad* to *Ulysses*. The city as center of consciousness is also a vast middenheap of discarded clichés whose retrieval forces upon them an archetypal character: "These fragments I have shored against my ruins" (T. S. Eliot, *The Waste Land*).

Joseph Frank discusses Dostoevski's *The House of the Dead* in terms which give stark iconic force to the division between the literate and the illiterate classes in a feudal society. To the peasant, the literate man is armored: " 'You gentry, iron-beaks, you devoured us.' "

Certain themes run through the *House of the Dead* like an obsessive refrain, appearing first in the initial four chapters—which serve as a kind of overture—and then echoing again and again in the later sections. The most persistent and all-pervasive theme of this kind is unquestionably that of the hatred of the Russian peasant for the educated class—the aristocrat or member of the "gentry," who was distinguished in Russia primarily by his education and his habits rather than by any more substantial attributes of status. . . . For only when a member of the gentry was forced to live among the peasants *as one of themselves* could he ever truly know their feelings. "They [the gentry] are divided from the peasants by an impassable gulf," he tells his readers, who all belong to the former category, "and this only becomes apparent when a *gentleman* is by force of external circumstances completely deprived of his former privileges and is transformed into a peasant."

In the electric age our senses and energies go outside as a new kind of collective and corporate environment. As such, this information environment of all-at-onceness and instant retrieval makes it difficult for the young to accept the specialized goals and fragmentary consciousness of nineteenth-century specialized man. Books like *The Catcher in the Rye* by J. D. Salinger, and movies like *The Graduate* suggest new roles for the young generation. Roles are somewhat antithetic to goals. In *The Graduate* Ben wears a deadpan tribal mask throughout. Confronted with his parents and their set, he is given the single inclusive image for life involvement: "In one word, Ben, *plastics*." "Plastics" has come to mean the phony, the ersatz. *The Graduate* simply presents Oedipus backward. The *agon* of the hero is to scrap his private identity and to plunge back into the tribal complex. He is seduced by his own "mother" and elopes with his own "sister."

Without incest, geneticists seem to say, there could be no species. Incest, of course, is radically conservative. In a world where all is change, creativity requires the conservation of mutations.

66

DOUBT

Dubito ergo sum was Descartes' original opening line of his *Discourse*. Berkeley replied: *Debeo ergo possum.* "Doubt" is from "double," or "echo," i.e., haunting doubts. Geoffrey Ashe tells us in *Arthur's Avalon* that the Celtic Church, unlike the Roman Church, was haunted by "a sense of something else." The oral culture is easily led to feel that something has been left out. Perhaps this is the origin of our feeling of *déjà vu*, the sense of having been "here" before. Gaps create the conditions of maximal participation.

Literate cultures tend to say "I cannot believe my eyes." The folk saying is "Seeing is believing, but touching is God's own truth." "Faith comes by hearing," and skepticism is inconceivable in a preliterate society. The technique of the doubt as a new cliché means of probing came into the twelfth century with the *Sic et Non* of Peter Abelard. His doubles marched along into the fifteenth century, when Nicholas of Cusa developed them into the doctrine of "learned ignorance" as a scientific technique of probe. Donne's *Biathanatos* is a masterpiece of irony in defense of suicide:

> Donne, I suppose, was such another
> Who found no substitute for sense,
> To seize and clutch and penetrate;
> Expert beyond experience,
>
> He knew the anguish of the marrow
> The ague of the skeleton;
> No contact possible to flesh
> Allayed the fever of the bone.
> —T. S. Eliot, "Whispers of Immortality"

Shakespeare, at the opening of *King Lear*, in the famous casuistical exchange with Cordelia, plays on the meaning of the word "nothing." It can mean "if you nothing knew," or "if you nothing me," if you destroy me, I'll destroy you. The daughters at the end of the first scene reverse "nothing" to "something," still with a destructive meaning: "We must do something, and i' the heat." Edgar supposes that the "something" which pursues him is the "foul fiend," a sort of nothing. It is left to Cordelia to "*nothing* nothing," to destroy destruction. In Hegel's thought the negation of negation is the Phoenix, the world as playhouse of forms.

EMOTION=SENTIMENT

The Emotion of Multitude—W. B. Yeats

The native act and figure of my heart.

> —*Othello*, Act I, Scene 1

Is this a dagger that I see before me?

> —*Macbeth*, Act II, Scene 1

For who would bear the whips and scorns of time . . .
That patient merit of the unworthy takes
When he himself might his quietus make
With a bare bodkin?

> —*Hamlet*, Act III, Scene 1

The motif must be sobby; it must proclaim: Everything is reduced to the sob, so we don't have to take the sob seriously, and above all we can be sure that a sudden, spontaneous variation will not make us aware of our resigned constant submission. Mass-man is irritated not only by traces of serious composition but also by signs of serious preparation on the part of the performer. Here again crops up his boundless conceit, which refuses to respect in another being a sign of nobility conferred by an education, in this case a musical one, and at the same time his self-annihilating modesty, which leads him to adore, his eyes popping out of his head, his idol or star, or whatever he might call the childishly

untrained performer of monotonous motifs. Therefore the true maxim
of the mass-man is this: I know I am a worm, but so is everyone
else. . . .

—Elémire Zolla, *The Eclipse of the Intellectual*

In his study of *Emotion* James Hillman notes:

> . . . the image of the knife raises fear only when that image
> has elements in common with instinct. . . . The image of the
> knife gives rise to emotion when it is part of an unconscious
> (repressed) complex impelled by instinctual forces. While
> for Jung, the complex to which the image of the knife is asso-
> ciated has a specific archetypal core which is the energetic
> drawing power of the complex and which makes the associa-
> tion, from an energetic point of view, possible. . . . *The image
> of the knife thus becomes a symbol.* It has a partly conscious
> and presented aspect and also a partly unconscious, non-
> presented and undefined aspect. . . . Or, in other terms, the
> conscious image is a *causa efficiens*, the unconscious image a
> *causa formalis* which unite in the symbol giving rise to emo-
> tion.

At the conclusion of his extensive survey of theories of emotion
James Hillman comments on the classical passage from the
Phaedrus of Plato on the wild horses of passion:

> We use the symbol of the Phaedrus myth because we have
> come to the end of rational explanation. The phenomenon of
> emotion is always partly outside consciousness. We can never
> know ultimately what emotion is, what it achieves or what
> sets it going. It remains a symbolic event; emotion is a "gift"
> said William James. But not, as he said, a gift either of flesh
> or spirit, but a gift of both flesh and spirit. Thus its danger
> for a gift can be a curse or a blessing, or a blessing in dis-
> guise. It can never be altogether understood because the

psyche as a whole is not grasped by consciousness alone. Emotion is always therefore a risk. To be known it must be lived. . . .

The word "symbol" is itself a *hyphen* situation which is relevant to Hillman's approach to the emotional complex. Briefly, all varieties of emotion can be considered as probes, e.g., the words "poignant" and "thrill" (from *thirl*, a hole, or piercing), "touchy," "edgy," "drained," etc.

Emotion as cliché-probe retrieves many older clichés from the "rag-and-bone shop." Joyce's phrase "a burning would is come to dance inane" is the essential theme of the *Wake*. This also expresses the impelling motive of change and innovation found in the Buddha fire sermon:

> Everything, Bhikkhus, is on fire. What everything, Bhikkhus, is on fire? The eye is on fire, the visible is on fire, the knowledge of the visible is on fire, the contact with the visible is on fire, the feeling which arises from the contact with the visible is on fire, be it pleasure, be it pain, be it neither pleasure nor pain. By what fire is it kindled? By the fire of lust, by the fire of hate, by the fire of delusion it is kindled, by birth age death pain lamentation sorrow grief despair it is kindled, thus I say. The ear . . . say. The nose . . . say. The tongue . . . say. The body . . . say. The mind . . . say.
>
> Knowing this, Bhikkhus, the wise man, following the Aryan path, learned in the law, becomes weary of the eye, he becomes weary of the visible, he becomes weary of the knowledge of the visible, he becomes weary of the contact of the visible, he becomes weary of the feeling which arises from the contact of the visible, be it pleasure, be it pain, be it neither pleasure nor pain. He becomes weary of the ear . . . pain. He becomes weary of the nose . . . pain. He becomes weary of the tongue . . . pain. He becomes weary of the body . . . pain. He becomes weary of the mind . . . pain.
>
> When he is weary of these things, he becomes empty of desire. When he is empty of desire, he becomes free. When he is free he knows that he is free, that rebirth is at an end,

that virtue is accomplished, that duty is done, and that there
is no more returning to this world; thus he knows.

—William Empson, *Collected Poems*

James Hillman continues: "The same distinction in kinds of
'motions of the soul' can be found in a Chinese book of life. There
is a movement based on the subject-object split. . . . External objects excite instinctual responses. But a second kind of motion which
starts from the 'heart' is objectless."

For most there is only the kind of emotion which refers to
our "animal being" which is "passionate because its motion is
locomotion. . . . Emotion is the hyphen, the functional connection
between subject and object. It is the Eros (flow of relation) across
the Chaos (gap)."

What Hillman does not stress is that "gap" or "interval" is the
space of *touch* or of tactility and involvement. The very word
"emotion" is a hyphenated gap, as it were. Hillman points to the
other aspect of ourselves, "that which we might say is particularly
our 'human being.' " This, then, is "passionate not only because
its motion is locomotion, but also because its motion and emotion
are part of the process of alteration, growth and decay. . . ." In
terms of the making of human identity we can say that emotion
is *the objectless movement of self-actualization.*"

Thus learning to tolerate emotion is a considerable discipline.
Abraham Maslow, in *Eupsychian Management* notes: "The calm
of the leader (I refuse to call him trainer which reminds me of
training bears, dogs) the way in which he can tolerate hostility
perhaps, or remain calm when someone weeps, is going counter to
the American mistrust of, and discomfort with, emotion, especially
deep emotion, whether negative or positive."

Maslow opens up the whole question of violence in entertainment and society:

> The whole discussion of hostility ought to be opened up
> much more richly by the sensitivity-training people . . . For
> instance, it could certainly be said, even in the few days I
> was there [Lake Arrowhead], that I saw people getting prac-
> tice in expressing hostility openly. This is a huge problem in

74

our society. Some people think that this is even the main problem confronting the psychoanalyst rather than what Freud took to be the main problem in 1890–1900 of repressed sexuality. . . .

Hostility and violence are directly associated with the retrieval of scrapped identity or threats to identity such as occur in periods of rapid transition. What Maslow is discussing here is stated by James Hillman:

> Another alternative of curing emotion through emotion is choosing one emotion to transform and re-order the others. Energetically expressed we tap the sources of all emotions if we live one fully. This is the way of *passion*. The emotion often recommended in the literature is love, but patriotism, racial hatred, ambition, sensual indulgence can serve as well, as long as the one chosen is lived fully and fanatically. . . .

ENVIRONMENT (AS CLICHÉ)

Those are mentally ill who, stricken by a serious disease, feel no pain.

—Hippocrates

It is dormition.

—James Joyce, *Finnegans Wake*

The city is the centre of paralysis.

—James Joyce

Sigfried Giedion devotes much of his Introduction *to Space, Time and Architecture* to the theme of "anonymous history," just as Hans Selye tackled the "pharmacology of dirt," or the whole environment, in *The Stress of Life*. Giedion approaches the entire man-made environment as architecture. Most of this environment is unintended and unplanned, or simply leftover junk from other periods. This anonymous history tends to be "invisible" much as John Cage's *Silence* consists of all the unintended noise of the environment, or as most poetry consists of all the "unintended meanings" or ambiguities.

In *Propaganda*, Jacques Ellul contends that it is the total culture in action that is propaganda, or teaching. Thus, real propaganda is environmental and invisible, like the perceptual bias of one's native language. The counterenvironments created by the artist serve to raise these hidden environments to the level of conscious appreciation.

Service environments which depend upon clichés or new technologies of retrieval, and which surround human totalities whether small or global in extent, become middenheaps or waste lands, or junkyards. One of the features of service environments is that two create less total service than one, or, in other words, the addition of service environments creates not increased service but a decrease of service. It is possible to consider human settlements or cities as dependent upon a multiplicity of service environments. A very early culture recently discovered in Anatolia depended almost entirely, as far as we can see from evidence at present available, upon a single grain (e.g., barley), and the same is true to some extent of much older cities such as those in Central America. Ordinarily cities, by addition of service environments, reduce service until it becomes drastically disservice. Additional service dislocates all the pre-existing ones, creating acute discomfort and disservice.

It is not insignificant that the great epics from Homer's *Iliad* to James Joyce's *Ulysses* have concerned the destruction of a city, or the destruction which a city has brought about. In Eliot's *The Waste Land* the city becomes a wilderness, and this is not so much figurative as literal. The accommodation of the citizens of *The Waste Land* to their service environment had robotized them: "I had not thought death had undone so many."

We add service environment to service environment in a city, that is to say, junkyard, and we end up with the most savage sort of jungle environment that we could possibly conceive. A professional explorer of jungles whose task was to capture dangerous animals and reptiles was asked whether a three-year-old child would be in more jeopardy in the most dangerous jungle in the world or playing on an urban sidewalk. He said, "The child would be in much greater danger on the city street. No creature in the jungle would harm him, although he might become hungry." One might query town planners when they try to surround the jungle of the city with super service environments or try to repair the service environments which, added together, have created the city. A service environment, by providing more or less impersonal, automatic services, kills or numbs the natural probing and exploring instincts of man. The city becomes superjungle.

A comparable situation to that of the town planner and the

ideal city is that of contrivers of ideal languages for international use. By removing all the superfluous junk, they present us with a sterile husk. It's as if some Herculean effort at "cleansing the Augean stables of speech" also got rid of the "rag-and-bone shop of the heart," so indispensable to the artist as the starting point of his creations.

Literary archetypalism has obscured Shakespeare's pervasive exploration of the meaning of culture. Most of his comedies, analogous to Sonnets 1–20, are concerned with husbandry in all senses. In the English histories Shakespeare sees the city as a cliché becoming feudal wasteland or junkpile, and feudalism itself as a product of the growth of the medieval city. Sonnet 124 shows him interfusing garden (cultural) and city (political) imagery. Love, he says,

> fears not policy, that heretic . . .
> But all alone stands hugely politique,
> That it nor grows with heat nor drowns with showers.

79

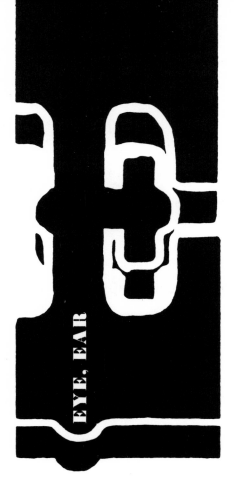

EYE, EAR

Formal patterns in America hold that when we want to express joy we laugh, to express grief we cry. . . . In Japan, as many an American discovered, laughter does not always mean that a person is happy. . . . Crying, too, may not necessarily mean that a person is sad. . . . Americans, on the other hand, have comparatively few technical and formal restrictions placed upon them but are loaded with informal ones. This means that Americans are apt to be quite inhibited, because they cannot state explicitly what the rules are. They can only point to them when they are violated.

81

—Edward T. Hall, *The Silent Language*

In any area that falls outside our visual culture, North Americans tend to be hung up in extreme complexities. For example, we have so many systems of measuring time in the West that "a well-known authority in the United States once stated it took the average child a little more than twelve years to master time."

For Ben Johnson, on the other hand, the acme of glamour was B.O., witness the last lines of "Drink to me only with thine eyes." Why the sudden need for a revival of aural values in print?

What is puzzling is that there should be such a sudden need for a revival of aural values in print. During most of this century such things as exclamation marks and italics (in Europe, letterspacing) have been found only in schoolgirl diaries. Our ideal has been measured, rational prose, or at

?

NEW PUNCTUATION
The double-duty interrobang

least the muscular prose of Hemingway and Dashiell Ham-
mett. Why, in the 1960s, is inflection suddenly necessary?

—*Toronto Daily Star*

It was Heisenberg in 1927 who introduced the idea of *resonance*
as the physical bond of the material "particles" of the universe.
The classic on the subject is *The Nature of the Chemical Bond* by
Linus Pauling.

Jacques Ellul observes in *Propaganda*: "When dialogue begins,
propaganda ends." His theme, that propaganda is not this or that
ideology but rather the action and coexistence of all media at
once, explains why propaganda is environmental and invisible.
The total life of any culture tends to be "propaganda" for this
reason. It blankets perception and suppresses awareness, making
the counterenvironments created by the artist indispensable to survival and freedom.

"Stile," says Shakespeare's contemporary, Puttenham, in his
The Arte of English Poesie, is "a constant and continual phrase or
tenour of speaking . . . therefore there be that have called stile the
image of man. . . ." The ancient saying had been: "Speak that I
may see thee." (George Stahmer's book of this title is on this
theme.)

"Tenour" is a technical term from music that Gray employs
in his "Elegy":

> Far from the madding crowd's ignoble strife,
>   Their sober wishes never learn'd to stray;
> Along the cool sequester'd vale of life
>   They kept the noiseless tenour of their way.

In the documentary history of the rise of the Third Reich very
little allusion is made to radio. Without radio there would have

82

been no Hitler, no tribal chieftains such as Churchill or Roosevelt. Without radio there would have been no world of jazz. Radio enabled the tribal and ear-oriented American Negro to extend to all the countries of the world the art form based on syncopation or symbolism. Beat is touch, and touch and the space of touch are interval. Interval requires closure, which creates rhythm. Not only, therefore, was jazz propagated by electric means but its form and structure are a direct reflex of electricity itself; that is, the world of the interval, not of the connection.

Literate people have great difficulty in approaching nonvisual spaces since they tend to accept the activity of the eye in isolation from the other spaces. Further, they assume that the Euclidean space created by the visual sense in isolation from the other senses is space itself. Under electric conditions, therefore, Western man is in a great state of confusion as he encounters the multiple forms of space generated by new technological environments. Literate and visually-oriented scientists in many fields, from mathematics to anthropology, make only the most oblique contact with other materials because of their unconscious visual orientation.

The return of the bardic tradition in the age of the Beatles and Joan Baez has created new problems in the study of English literature. Much modern poetry today is written to be sung. The boundaries between the written and the oral are becoming very elusive.

The range of situations affected by the shift from eye to ear is unlimited. It includes William Empson's *Seven Types of Ambiguity*, which opens: "An ambiguity, in ordinary speech, means something very pronounced, and as a rule witty or deceitful."

The first example of ambiguity occurs when "only one statement is effective in several ways at once." This is simply another way of saying that verbal echo has once more become relevant. From a literal point of view, language so considered is a "rag-and-bone shop" of incomplete utterance. The incomplete building, like the semi-demolished one, holds the attention more than the complete form, as in:

Bare ruined choirs where late the sweet birds sang.
—Shakespeare, Sonnet lxxiii

Talent Rides Only in a Hackneyed Vehicle

Many of the more contemporary approaches to the theory of genres were, of course, anticipated by Shakespeare. Professor Frye has put the matter with mathematical succinctness: "The basis of generic distinction in literature appears to be the radical of presentation."

Hamlet, also, goes to the heart of the matter in his encounter with the players: "Then came each actor on his ass." Polonius is more circumstantial in classifying the modes in which, as Professor Frye says, "words may be acted in front of a spectator, . . ." Polonius retrieves his archetypal forms from a much larger store of traditional rhetoric than Professor Frye dips into:

> POLONIUS: The best actors in the world, either for tragedy, comedy, history, pastoral, pastoral-comical, historical-pastoral, tragical-historical, tragical-comical-historical-pastoral, scene individable, or poem unlimited; Seneca cannot be too heavy, nor Plautus too light. For the law of writ and the liberty, these are the only men.
>
> —*Hamlet*, Act II, Scene 2

Working entirely from the medium of the printed word, Professor Frye has developed a classification of literary forms that ignores not only the print process as it created a special type of writer and audience, but all other media as well:

> Criticism, we note resignedly in passing, has no word for the individual member of an author's audience, and the word "audience" itself does not really cover all genres, as it is slightly illogical to describe the readers of a book as an audience.

In this century the effect of nonprint media on literature has been as extensive as it has been on psychology and anthropology, from which Professor Frye derives many of his categories of classification. *Time* magazine for March 7, 1969, discusses the collapse of psychoanalysis in the age of the inner trip. The *Time* editors have no idea of why the "yung and easily freudened" are now as passé as "Getting Gertie's Garter." The arrival of "tribulation" (retribalized man) in the TV age has ended the condition of personal isolation that evoked the attentions of Sigmund Freud. E. R. Leach in *A Runaway World?* explains how the railway helped to scatter the large kinship groupings of European and English society in the later nineteenth century. The "nuclear" or isolated family of mom-pop-and-the-kids put one-to-one strains on individuals that were unbearable. "Sex" also separated out from the general social life in the mechanical age. Today, with much greater speed-up of travel and information, the fragmentation of social life has reversed into corporate forms again. Unisex is not homosexuality but complementarity. The classifications of psychoanalysis are irrelevant to the TV generation.

Anthropology has undergone a similar hardening of its categories since movie cameras have been put into the hands of "natives" so they can record their own arts and ceremonies. George Puttenham, in *The Arte of English Poesie*, observed in 1589 that standard English could be taken to be the "usuall speach of the Court and that of London and the shires lying about London within forty myles, and not much above, . . . but herein we are already ruled by the English Dictionaries and other books written by learned men, . . ." (Book 3, Chapter 4.)

The legal world is full of theatrical genres, and it is easy to illustrate from F. W. Maitland:

> . . . English law knows a certain number of forms of action, each with its own uncouth name, a writ of right, an assize of novel disseisin or of *morte d'ancestor*, a writ of entry *sur disseisin* in the *per* and *cui*, a writ of *besaiel*, of *quare impedit*, an action of covenant, debt, detinue, replevin, trespass, assumpsit, ejectment, case. This choice is not merely a

choice between a number of queer technical terms, it is a choice between methods of procedure adapted to cases of different kinds.

However, medieval scholars point out that it is quite impossible to have a medieval dictionary, since authors defined their terms in the act of writing. Looking at this aspect of continual change in language, Pope observed: "Such as Chaucer is, will Dryden be." It was this flux in language that many felt Dr. Johnson's dictionary (1755) constrained.

By ignoring the oral tradition of both preliterate and postliterate cultures, Professor Frye sets up a system of classifications that apply to a recent segment of human technology and culture—a segment that is rapidly dissolving. If we are restricted to Professor Frye's categories of printed literature, the entire history of genre from Homer to the present—a subject enriched by thousands of poets and scholars in explicit commentary on their works—is resignedly ignored.

87

Today the entire world of rock poetry and of the related forms of jazz, of song and speech and dance, has created a complex world of genre which no professor of literature can ignore if he has any concern about maintaining contact with his students. The interests of literature are not really served by ignoring its rivals.

Anthropology, psychology, sociology have all provided contemporary man with new genres of visual literature, and he is, moreover, endlessly fascinated with these. Inner-tripping began with the Symbolists, long before Jung and Freud—with Coleridge, De Quincy, Baudelaire and Poe, with Lewis Carroll. Today the genre is as wide as psychedelia and has specific terms for members of the body and physical and mental postures such as "head" and "acid head"; "bag," "groove," and "into"; "nark," "busted," "bummer," "spaced," "strung out," "high," and "stoned," etc. Still another posture is indicated by a preference for acronyms in identifying drugs, as STP, LBJ, THC, LSD.

The world of *The Silent Language* explored by Edward T. Hall has opened up the world of genres. The Elizabethan malcontent, Vindici style, has proliferated into the modern whodunit, perhaps the major literary genre of our century. W. H. Auden begins his essay on the genre of the whodunit under the title of "The Guilty Vicarage" and with the epigraph: "I had not known sin, but by the law" (Romans 7:7).

A Confession

> For me, as for many others, the reading of detective stories is an addiction like tobacco or alcohol. The symptoms of this are: firstly, the intensity of the craving—if I have any work to do, I must be careful not to get hold of a detective story for, once I begin one, I cannot work or sleep till I have finished it. Secondly, its specificity—the story must conform to certain formulas (I find it very difficult, for example, to read one that is not set in rural England). And, thirdly, its immediacy. I forget the story as soon as I have finished it, and have no wish to read it again. If, as sometimes happens, I start reading one and find after a few pages that I have read it before, I cannot go on.

Mr. Auden is a classifier who misses the main point about the process of involvement of the whodunit. Like the Symbolist poem which requires much involvement, it is written backwards. However, he does give some heed to the readers of this genre as part of this definition: "I suspect that the typical reader of detective stories is, like myself, a person who suffers from a sense of sin." He does find the genre excludes him from other forms of "daydream" literature.

The espionage thriller is a variant of the whodunit, dramatizing the decision-making process at the highest levels of power. The most fascinating of all Shakespeare's tragedies, *Hamlet*, is an anticipation of this espionage and counterespionage thriller—this spy story to end all spy stories. The quest is both inner and outer, as exemplified today by Agatha Christie in *Murder after Hours*:

> She smiled at him.
> "Is it a bargain, M. Poirot?"
> It was quite an effort for Hercule Poirot to say, "No, Madame, it is not a bargain."

He wanted—he wanted, very badly, to let the whole thing drop—simply because Lucy Angkatell asked him to do so.

The detective story in which the characters do not have cartoon-like bounding lines, but are given the realistic treatment of a conventional novel, is a very strange hybrid. For one thing, the narrative is scrambled in the detective story; it is deliberately interrupted and lacking in important connectives that the psychological novel relies upon to reveal character. When character is pushed to a conventional extreme and provided with an inclusive bounding line that contains all facets of the character at once, the narrative function is displaced.

In his *The Old Drama and the New*, William Archer traces the opposite process by which, in the history of drama, characterization moved from the Elizabethan stock types to nineteenth-century pictorial realism. His book appeared shortly after *Ulysses* and *The Waste Land*, in which works there is a sudden return of iconic stock characters. Stephen Dedalus, Leopold Bloom, and Gerty McDowell are flat, iconic forms, filled with and formed by age-old collective experiences. It is a paradox explored in this book that the flat cliché is an enormously richer and deeper form than anything that can be achieved by pictorial realism and the most delicate shades of chiaroscuro. It is the same in painting. The flat icon has multitudinous layers of significance, whereas the three-dimensional perspective illusion necessarily specializes in one facet at a time.

The figure of the revenger in Elizabethan drama, the figure of the malcontent, is a retrieved form of the medieval and feudal lord. The dissolution of medieval social organization meant the release of the individual from depth involvement in social roles. This is exactly the process by which realism supplanted stylized and iconic social roles such as appear in Chaucer's "Prologue." The social emergence of the individual from the corporate role was a parallel to the rise of realism in psychology and narrative. Realism is specialism and fragmentation. Whatever diminishes fragmentation also diminishes realism. That is why electric circuitry, in creating new integral patterns of social organization, also re-creates iconic patterns in daily life, as well as in the arts.

If the Elizabethan malcontent was a figure of social distress and dissolution, so is the modern sleuth, or detective. This figure looks two ways. He has one orientation toward the recent past of individual self-reliance and initiative. But as a researcher and a prober he has another orientation in the present. He is thus quite ambiguous. Hamlet, too, has a double orientation, like the whole of Shakespeare's vision. On the one hand there is a deep commitment to the feudal past and its hierarchies of values, but there is also the awareness of a self-conscious and doubtful present. In our own time the same ambiguity is dramatized between the conscious and the unconscious, between the individual and the collective. In fifth-century Athens a similar ambiguity existed between the oral and mythic world of Homer and Hesiod and the new literate individualism. This uneasy state appears everywhere in Greek drama and in modern symbolism. Zolla comments:

> But unlike Melville, Poe tried to adjust to the times and invent new genres suited to the new style of existence. Thus he wrote in a letter to Longfellow in 1841: "I need not call your attention to the signs of the times in respect to Magazine literature. You will admit that the tendency of the age lies in this way—so far at least as regards the lighter letters. The brief, the condensed, and the easily circulated will take the place of the diffuse, the ponderous, and the inaccesible."

Perhaps superior in scope and popularity to the whodunit is the Western. Owen Wister's *The Virginian* may have been a prototype. The theme is the quest for identity on the frontier between two worlds. The Virginian is a stereotype, representative of the Western civilized man, detached, poised, and aristocratic. On the frontier, everyone is a nobody and must prove himself each day. He has no "place" in the world. Thus the Western is a paradigm of the condition of man in a rapidly changing or a growing society.

The ritualistic and functional costume of the cowboy, worn in an environment little affected by human artifacts, has made the Western a natural form for the media of both movie and TV.

One of the most successful genres of this age is the book title itself as a "youdunit." It involves the reader in such titles as: *Time and Western Man*; *The Revolt of the Masses*; *The Managerial Revolution*; *The Organization Man*; *The Affluent Society*; *Time, Space and Architecture*; *The Impossible Theatre*; *Management and Machiavelli*; *Gods, Graves and Scholars*; *The Hidden Persuaders*; *Doctors and Drugs*; *The Death of God*; *The Double Helix*; *The Biological Time Bomb*. Replacing the encyclopedias of earlier centuries, such books are all "guides to understanding." Jay's *Management and Machiavelli*, for example, uses the same overall pattern as Joyce's *Ulysses*. Retrieving the figure of Machiavelli, it uses this as a probe of modern management techniques. Its relevance with respect to managerial practices is, however, subordinated to its attack on the reader's ego. It is an ego-inflating drug, and it is as such that it explores a particular group of readers.

In *TV Guide* Marya Mannes refers to another genre and asks, "When will soap operas grow up?" As a companion to the horse opera, the soap opera is a significant genre. Unlike the rugged pioneering Western, the soap opera, in her words,

91

> . . . concerns itself basically with one kind of America: the comfortable suburban life of white, middle-class Protestants, the homes always impeccably neat and ultraconservative, the men either lawyers, doctors, small-business men or newspaper types, the women always perfectly coiffed and smartly attired, the forces of good and the forces of evil neatly opposed, love finally triumphant over obstacles that would have mired Eros himself.

Miss Mannes thinks that we ought to have a new genre based on the ideals of nineteenth-century liberal literati, which would, of course, deal with the perfectly coiffed woman sitting at the executive desk. In a word, she is a student activist, a candidate for a sit-in.

Peter Farb, in his study *Man's Rise to Civilization* discusses the Iroquois' false face, of which he says, "The false faces really should not be regarded as masks, since they were not intended to hide anything." What he says is interesting but inadequate, since he goes on to speak of the masks as "portraits into which the supernatural has made itself manifest."

The author of a *Newsweek* entry sees more deeply, however:

MIMIC MASTERS

A good mimic can latch onto a personality and wear it like a suit of clothes. Sometimes, it's catching a voice, such as the raspy tones of John Wayne that creak like a brand-new Western saddle. . . .

The same approach serves for a remoter scene:

The mythical ancestors of the Australian aborigines are man and animal simultaneously, or sometimes man and plant. These figures, as we know already, are called totems: there is a kangaroo, an opossum and an emu totem. Each of these is man and animal at the same time; it acts both as a man and as a particular animal, and is regarded as the ancestor of both.

What are we to make of these archaic figures? What actually is it that they represent? If we are to understand them we must remember that they are regarded as beings belonging to an age of myth, a period in which metamorphosis was the common gift of all creatures and constantly practised. It has often been pointed out how *fluid* the world was then. Not only could a man transform himself into anything, but he also had the power to transform others. In the universal flux certain figures stand out, which are nothing but particular metamorphoses fixed and made permanent. The figure which men cling to, which becomes a life-giving tradition enacted and spoken of over and over again, is not the abstraction of an animal species, not Kangaroo or Emu, but a kangaroo who is also a man, or a man who at will can become an emu. . . .

The *mask* is distinguished from all the other end-states of transformation by its rigidity. In place of the varying and continuous movement of the face it presents the exact opposite: a perfect fixity and sameness. Man's perpetual readiness for transformation is clearly expressed in the mobility of his face. The play of his features is far richer and more varied

92

than that of any animal and he has, too, the richest experience of transformation. It is inconceivable how many changes a face can undergo in the course of a single hour. If one had time to study all the movements and moods which pass over it one would be astonished at the number of seminal transformations it reveals.

One of the largest areas of genre study and practice concerned *decorum* or the propriety of different forms of dress and expression in different circumstances. This is handled succinctly and definitively by Quintilian (c. 35–c. 100 A.D.). His institutes of oratory put the matter as follows:

There is another threefold division, whereby, it is held, we may differentiate three styles of speaking, all of them correct. The first is termed the plain, the second grand and forcible, and the third intermediate. The nature of these three styles is, broadly speaking, as follows. The first would seem best adapted for instructing, the second for moving, and the third for charming or, as others would have it, conciliating the audience; for instruction the quality most needed is acumen, for conciliation gentleness, and for stirring the emotions force. Consequently it is mainly in the plain style that we shall state our facts and advance our proofs, though it should be borne in mind that this style will often be sufficiently full in itself without any assistance whatever from the other two. The intermediate style will have more frequent recourse to metaphor and will make more attractive use of figures, while it will introduce alluring digressions, will be neat in rhythm and pleasing in its reflections: its flow, however, will be gentle, like that of a river whose waters are clear, but overshadowed by the green banks on either side. But he whose eloquence is like to some great torrent that rolls down rocks and "disdains a bridge" and carves out its own banks for itself, will sweep the judge from his feet, struggle as he may, and force him to go whither he bears him. . . This is he that will inspire anger or pity, and while he speaks the judge will call upon the gods and weep, following him wherever he sweeps him from one emotion to another, and no longer asking merely for instruc-

93

tion. Wherefore if one of these three styles has to be selected to the exclusion of the others, who will hesitate to prefer this style to all others, since it is by far the strongest and the best adapted to the most important cases? For Homer himself assigns to Menelaus an eloquence, terse and pleasing, exact (for that is what is meant by "making no errors in words") and devoid of all redundance, which qualities are virtues of the first type: and he says that from the lips of Nestor flowed speech sweeter than honey, than which assuredly we can conceive no greater delight: but when he seeks to express the supreme gift of eloquence possessed by Ulysses he gives a mighty voice and a vehemence of oratory equal to the snows of winter in the abundance and the vigour of its words. "With him then," he says, "no mortal will contend, and men shall look upon him as on a god." It is this force and impetuosity that Eupolis admires in Pericles, this that Aristophanes compares to the thunderbolt, this that is the power of true eloquence.

94

Whereas the classical epic—the "tribal encyclopedia," as Eric Havelock calls it in his *Preface to Plato*—was concerned with the group, the "city," little epic was *aitiological*, concerned with natural causes and natural science. It was, therefore, for pagan men the world of the gods and the natural forces of the universe. Ovid's *Metamorphoses* corresponds to *I Ching*.

In the Middle Ages and the Renaissance the pastoral form of the little epic was primarily theological, as in Dante and Spenser and Milton. In modern poetry the concern with cause and effect in a society of rapid change brought the little epic form back into prominence in Pound, Eliot, and Joyce, among others.

The only extensive study of this form is Marjorie Crump's *The Epyllion from Theocritus to Ovid*, which is discussed in the Introduction to *Tennyson* by Marshall McLuhan:

> . . . The so-called art of the little epic (the idyll and epyllion) was a late Greek form associated with magical rituals. It was especially cultivated by Theocritus, who was Tennyson's favorite poet. Theocritus and the Alexandrian school were directly responsible for "the new poetry" of Catullus, Ovid,

and Virgil. The work of Theocritus, Catullus, Ovid, and Virgil, masters of the epyllion, needs to be known for any deep understanding of Tennyson's technique in narrative poetry. But the discontinuous technique of the epyllion is equally the clue to the art form of *Dubliners*, of *The Waste Land*, and of *The Cantos*.

Professor Crump describes the epyllion as follows:

> ". . . a short narrative poem. The length may and does vary considerably, but an epyllion seems never to have exceeded the length of a single book, and probably the average length was four to five hundred lines. The subject is sometimes merely an incident in the life of an epic hero or heroine, sometimes a complete story, the tendency of the author being to use little-known stories or possibly even to invent new ones. The later Alexandrians and Romans preferred love stories and usually concentrated the interest on the heroine. . . . The dramatic form is frequently employed, and it is usual to find at least one long speech."

. . . Whereas the cyclic epic, as in Homer, moves on the single narrative plane of individual spiritual quest, the little epic as written by Ovid, Dante, Joyce, and Pound is "the tale of the tribe." That is to say, it is not so much a story of the individual quest for perfection as it is a history of collective crime and punishment, an attempt to justify the ways of God to man. From this point of view "In Memoriam," like Petrarch's *Sonnets*, is a seasonal cycle of little epics or idylls in the form of the individual quest. And the *Idylls of the King* is the collective quest, the tale of the tribe. The twelve idylls follow the cycle of the zodiac, each book corresponding faithfully to the traditional character of the twelve "houses" of the zodiac. By following this traditional zodiacal track Tennyson was able over a long period to compose his twelve idylls in any order he found convenient.

The pattern of collective quest lends the prominent salvation note to the *Idylls of the King* and explains his philosophy of history. "The Coming of Arthur" is thus the coming of the culture-hero, and Arthur's struggles with the demonic earth powers are the theme of the cycle. The masculine-feminine duality of most of Tennyson's *Idylls of the King* may have been suggested to him by the similar aspect of each house of the zodiac. For each planet's day home is located in a positive masculine sign, and its night home in a negative or feminine sign.

The epyllion is a liturgical ceremonial ritual in origin, pastoral, seasonal, and collective as indicated in the opening words of *The Waste Land*: "April is the cruelest month." The meeting with Stetson which follows draws attention to the typical use of double mask of the interface plot and subplot, of the putting on of two audiences. Eliot had stressed the importance of this form in his essay "*Ulysses*, Order, and Myth," in which he draws attention to use of this double form by both Yeats and Joyce. He also insists that it is the only means of giving order to the anarchy of our time. The little epic, like the cyclic epic before it, incorporated massive erudition. In our time it does this by esoteric allusion and compression, retrieving folk clichés obscurely and ironically.

Theater, with its multimedia, music, dance, song, acting, mime, etc., is obviously a multiprobe, multigenre experience. What this means is that a diversity of audiences are appealed to or probed or transformed at the same time. It may be that allegory can be approached as multigenre. *Everyman*, for example, probes both the ordinary commercial member of late medieval society and his clerical advisor. Dante's *Comedy* probes three or four levels of reader or audience. First, Dante addresses himself to the monastic, next to his fellow Italians or Florentines, and third to the classical scholar. The modern allegory, like Kafka's *The Trial* or *The Castle*, again probes both the totalitarian and the anti-totalitarian reader. Most works of art have a quasi-allegorical quality.

It would be easy to enumerate many contemporary genres such as that indicated by Henry James and his "trapped spectator" or Kafka and his "prisoners." Utopias and anti-Utopias abound as genre. The movie world has produced many genres related to heroes, villians, fools. Harold Rosenberg in *The Tradition of the*

New points out how Marx characterizes "the historical drama" that "would be played without costumes, without mistaken identities or mistaken roles, without absolutes," by the proletariat of Karl Marx. In actuality, Marx as a genre-maker is really summing up the features of the group image which he is exploring, the proletariat.

One of the most prolific genres of our time has come from the return to the mask or image so necessary to the corporate life of business and politics. The word *persona* was the name of the Roman actor's mask, from which we derive the idea of the human person. Puttenham has an interesting note on the mask in *The Arte of English Poesie*, Book 1, Chapter 14:

> The old comedy had used masks, but the new comedy played bareface till one *Roscius Gallus*, the most excellent player among the Romanes brought up these vizards which we see at this day used partly to supply the want of players, when there were moe parts than there were persons, or that it was not thought meek to trouble and pester princes' chambers with too many folkes. Now by the chaunge of a vizard one man might play the king and carter, the old nurse and the young damsell, the marchant and the souldier or any other part he listed very conveniently.

97

The world of Ezra Pound is based upon a recovery of the idea of mask as a pattern of energy. Thus any poem, painting, novel is a mask of the writer worn by the audience.

Wyndham Lewis invoked the same principle in his idea of the Vortex, where artist merges with *homo ludens*, a sort of playboy of the West End world:

> The Fine Arts today survive on the same basis (or that will soon be the case) as the Art of the hunter or *sportsman*. Hunting, the supreme art and business of primitive life, survived in our civilization as the most delightful pastime and a coveted privilege. So the fine arts, corresponding to no present need that a variety of industries cannot answer more effectively, the last survivals of the *hand* against the *machine*, but beaten by the machine in every contest involving a practical issue, must, if they survive at all, survive as a sport, as a

privilege of the wealthy, negligently indulged in—not any longer as an object of serious devotion.

The sport of hunting either large or small game is the symbol of an idle and strictly useless life; and today the fox-hunter and the painter or poet are in the same category. All that is necessary is for the fox-hunter to take to painting pictures and writing verse, and the close association of these two occupations in the public mind will be effected.

Had the primitive hunter been presented suddenly with machine-guns, with which he could mow down his game in droves, he would not have troubled to practise his lonely and difficult art any more. Similarly, had the peruvian potters been accommodated with the resources of a Staffordshire factory for producing pots, they would have immediately abandoned their archaic wheel. Since men in the aggregate, however, are made by their occupation, both the potter and the hunter would deteriorate, become parasitic on their machines, and upon the engineer and inventor. But in neither case would that appear to them as a consideration of an order to appeal to a man or woman of the world.

A business that survives as a sport does so only when it has some pleasure-value or vanity-value. Shooting or trapping other animals has these values. Also the pictorial representation of objects, the composing of music and performing on musical instruments, singing, literary composition, verbal dexterity and so forth, possess great pleasure-value and great vanity-value.

In future probably what are now still "artists" by profession (for there are still people who on identity cards describe themselves in that way) will form a class similar to that of gamekeepers, huntsmen, horse trainers, sculptors' ghosts, and printers' devils. They will be the people who will keep the game, but not shoot at it—rear the horse, but not ride it. The actual *act of art* (whereby a picture is finally produced with delight, or a song sung with unction) will become of the same character as the laying of a foundation-stone, or let us say the ceremonious fixing of the last tile upon the roof, or the driving of the last rivet into the flank of the beflagged ship.

The interplay among masks of energy awakens our awareness of the earliest antecedents. This is the theme of "Tradition and the Individual Talent" by T. S. Eliot—that the advent of new form affects all earlier forms. Joyce employs the "magazine wall" for alerting us to this process: "by the butt of the magazine wall/Where the maggies seen all." This wall is a burrow, or barrow, of vast variety and accumulation. A magazine is a storehouse of ammunition as well. When the pitch of this wall achieves a certain gradient, Humpty-Dumpty tumbles off the wall. Humpty-Dumpty is the mask of the integral and ordered unity of tradition (and the structured sensorium) that recurrently crashes with the advent of major technological change. The fragments are reassembled through the flowing energies of the "heroine" A.L.P.

Another theme of the *Wake* that helps in the understanding of the paradoxical shift from cliché to archetype is "pastimes are past times." The dominant technologies of one age become the games and pastimes of a later age. In the twentieth century the number of past times that are simultaneously available is so vast as to create cultural anarchy. When all the cultures of the world are simultaneously present, the work of the artist in the elucidation of form takes on new scope and new urgency. Most men are pushed into the artist role. The artist cannot dispense with the principle of doubleness and interplay since this kind of hendiadys-dialogue is essential to the very structure of consciousness, awareness, and autonomy.

George Puttenham (Book 3) cites several modes of the figures of masking, beginning with "hypotiposis" or "the counterfait representation" and "prosopographia." He notes: ". . . the visage speach and countenance of any person absent or dead; and this kind of representation is called counterfait countenance: . . . as our poet 'Chaucer' doth in his Canterbury Tales set foorth the sumner, Pardoner. . . ." Next he mentions "prosopopeia. . . . If ye will attribute any humane quality, as reason or speach to dombe creatures or other sensible things, . . ." After mentioning "chronographia" and "typographia" he cites "pragmato graphia" or "counterfait" action: "The handling of any business with the circumstances belonging thereunto has the manner of a battell, a

99

feast, a marriage, a buriall or any other matter that lieth in feat and activity: . . ."

The familiar phrase "maskings and dumb shows" included a great range of verbal and nonverbal genres. Today the Chinese poster-newspaper or enacting of daily events nonverbally in the streets tends to merge with sit-ins and teach-ins and many other uses of public places for dramatic action.

The writer and the actor both have to "put on" their audiences. The nighttown ("Circe") episode in *Ulysses* as a virtuoso exhibition of contemporary masking makes multileveled demands upon the attention of its readers.

Even the new instruments of sensory measurement draw attention to the iconic aspects of visual perception. An X-ray radiologist looks at his images as if he were handling them. Dr. Llewellyn-Thomas, using the movie head-camera, reveals how nearly the eye tends to mime the patterns of abstract art in its encounters with the world. Most of our ideas of the visual are not related to visual action so much as to the conceptual and the cultural residues of traditional learning. Dr. Llewellyn-Thomas notes:

100

> Harley Parker and I recorded and compared the visual behaviour of an artist and a nonartist as they examined a series of paintings. The pitfalls in reporting such subjective studies are obvious, but there seems no doubt that many painters are highly successful in directing the movements of our eyes. The artist viewer appeared more sensitive to this, particularly with respect to more abstract pictures. The eyes of both men, however, were drawn to discontinuities, including the edges of the picture itself.
>
> This agrees with recent neurophysiological findings that contours and borders, such as those in a checkerboard, are strong stimuli of the evoked voltages that can be measured in the brain when such items are presented to the eye. This might also be expected from the fact that the border defines the shape and is a key information element in a scene. The visual pull of such borders may constitute an impediment if the viewer is searching for a low-contrast feature, such as an abnormality in an X-ray film of the chest. Edward L. Lans-

down and I recorded the eye movements of a group of student radiologists as they inspected a selection of chest X-rays. Our records showed that the students had carefully examined the edges of the heart and the margins of the lung fields, and indeed these are important regions for signs of disease. But large areas of the lung fields were never inspected by most of the students in the group, even though they thought they had scanned the films adequately.

On the other hand, Shakespeare too had noted the effects of visual stress in his own time. The new grammar of abstraction and pictorial verisimilitude he recognized as fictions of the painter's eye:

Mine eye hath play'd the painter and hath stell'd
Thy beauty's form in table of my heart;
My body is the frame wherein 'tis held,
And perspective it is best painter's art,
For through the painter must you see his skill, . . .

101

Yet eyes this cunning want to grace their art,
They draw but what they see, know not the heart.

—Shakespeare, Sonnet xxiv

By accelerating our Western technology we have gone Oriental on all fronts. That is, the new high speeds of movement of both hardware and software enable us to discover, even in visual space itself, the intervals and resonances which also underlie much of the Oriental modes of being and art:

The idea embodied in the Chinese symbol for space is thus quite different from the idea embodied in the Western word "space." To give a quick and over-simplified contrast, let us say: the West speaks of "space"; the East speaks of "spacing." Having said that, we might do well to look at the nature of the languages involved.

The Chinese symbols are ideograms, that is to say, graphs of an idea, and therefore are not pictures of abstract things or nouns, as we know them in Western linguistics, but actions, shorthand images of natural process and operations. . . .

The idea of nature is not an abstract thing in isolation which can be called a noun. In the Western sense, nouns are only end points, or goals, which are a condition of our literal culture; they are the interesting points of events, the steps involved in a process which is a part of the perspective of life. Likewise, an abstract movement, corresponding to a verb in grammar, is impossible in nature. The Chinese ideogram makes no separation. Things are, in that they are in movement; they are alive and flexible.

The Western argument of form following function, or function following form, is impossible. In the East, form and function are one and the same; form is the combination of space and function, and as function or space change, so does form, and therefore form is never fixed but is temporal. . . .

Negative "Ma" is related to the embarrassment of seeing or being seen. This is related to Japanese ethics whereby the system of obligation, "giri" and "on," imply that the individual is non-existent by himself but is rather a part of a greater whole of which the "Ma" is a network of obligations. . . .

The Japanese sense of "Ma" is therefore related to the experience of the person perceiving the arrangement of various elements rather than the arrangement of the elements themselves. "Ma" is the attitude of the mind created by the external distribution of symbols.

It is interesting . . . to note that before the latter part of the 19th century, there was no word for "logic."* However, with the introduction of Western thought, the word "Rogikku" (Japanese pronunciation for logic) was adopted. Until this time, the pattern of un-logical thinking called "Haragei" was the rejection of rationalism and denial of logical thinking. The Japanese preferred to settle problems emotionally rather than to apply rationality.

The "Ma" of architecture is defined in the dictionary as the spacing between pillars, "Hashira To Hashira No Aida."

* NOTE: There did exist a type of Buddhist logic which originated in India, and travelled through China and Korea to Japan (Ronri). This was quite different from Western "Logic."

I should like to demonstrate this graphically by saying, that if we were to take two sheets of paper and cover one with black, then erase white patches from the black, in what I choose to call a cavity approach, we would see the Western idea of space in architecture—static and secure.

—Fred and Barbro Thompson, "The Japanese Concept of *Ma*"

Eliot's familiar passage about the Chinese jar ("Burnt Norton" V) draws attention to the same aspect of space as interval. The reader can find a full discussion of the resonance of the chemical bond in Linus Pauling's *The Nature of the Chemical Bond.*

One of the numerous genres omitted from this discussion is mentioned in the Introduction to *Candide* by Lester G. Crocker, who said: "Voltaire was the master of the 'philosophical tale,' a genre designed for the popularizing of ideas." (It's a very waggish genre indeed!) "His genius raised it from the level of propaganda to that of literature."

The age swarmed with these tales, from *Gulliver's Travels* to Mary Shelley's *Frankenstein.* They tend to melt quickly, like those stories of C. P. Snow. W. S. Gilbert indicates that the perfect matching of crime and punishment transforms penance into joy. This mystery had eluded the speculations of Voltaire and the probers of optimism and pessimism in the eighteenth century.

Adam Smith in *The Wealth of Nations* sets up a similar principle of balance or equilibrium as a rule for universal happiness and contentment in his Theory of Free Trade. "If only human meddlers will avoid tampering with the cosmic harmonies, all will be for the best in the best of all possible worlds." This theory of equilibrium, resulting from maximal collision, is heralded in Liebnitzian monadology and became the principle of the Democratic ballot box, i.e., if everybody will allow his opinion to conflict with everybody's opinion, perfect representation and political harmony result. The difficulty arises from the human temptation to improve on these cosmic arrangements of conflict which insures the maximum of human happiness. Gilbert handles the entire matter better than Sartre or these gloomy moralists. Their failure is to ignore the mechanism of the universe in favor of its content. In its definition of "dialect," the unabridged edition of *The Random*

House Dictionary of the English Language points to the group-forming characteristics of dialects.

> 1. Ling. a variety of language that is distinguished from other varieties of the same language by the features of phonology, grammar, and vocabulary, and by its use by a group of speakers who are set off from others geographically or socially. 2. a provincial, rural, or socially distinct variety of a language that differs from the standard language, esp. when considered as substandard.

John Locke quite obviously thought of standard language as a service environment, for he observes that

> . . . The comfort and advantage of society not being to be had without communication of thoughts, it was necessary that man should find out some external sensible signs, whereof these invisible ideas, which his thoughts are made up of, might be made known to others. . . .

Though it is helpful to think of a dialect as a genre probing or retrieving a group, in order to understand the distinction between a language and a dialect it is still more useful to think of genre as acting like dialects in the formation of groups. A mask as a genre is the group-face, a dialect as genre is the group-speech. Conversely, a genre is dialect, mask, dress, or any other group furniture. In a world where the communications satellite is the latest and all-embracing service environment, and where service environment upon service environment operates to produce a milieu of total irresponsibility, the importance of the group-creating characteristics of genre can hardly be overestimated. If so, and if a genre is a dialect, then Eric Partidge's etymology of this word is significant:

> *dialegesthai*, to converse, has pp *dialektos*, which, used as n, becomes L *dialectus* (gen *-ūs*), EF-F *dialecte*, E *dialect* . . .

(This etymology is taken from Partidge's *Origins*, under the entry "legend," which collects together words derived from the Latin *legere*, "to gather (esp. fruit), hence to collect, to assemble.")

Leo Rosten's *The Joys of Yiddish* shows how the interface or dialogue between two cultures can produce a rich new "Yinglish." Yinglish has provided a comic mask of subtle psychological nuances of contempt and humor for countless performers both on and off stage. Let Mr. Rosten speak for himself:

> Every so often I run across the statement that *Webster's Unabridged Dictionary* contains 500 Yiddish words. I do not know if this is true, and I certainly doubt that anyone actually counted them. For my part, I am surprised by the number of Yiddish words, thriving beautifully in everyday English, that are *not* in *Webster's*, nor in other dictionaries of the English language—including the incomparable thirteen-volume *Oxford English Dictionary*. . . .
>
> Take the popular usage of the suffix, *-nik*, to convert a word into a label for an ardent practitioner or devotee of something: How could we manage without such priceless coinages as *beatnik* and *peacenik*? *The New York Times* recently dubbed Johann Sebastian's acolytes "Bachniks"; some homosexuals dismiss non-homosexuals as *straightniks*; . . .

105

COLLOQUIAL USES IN ENGLISH OF YIDDISH LINGUISTIC DEVICES

But words and phrases are not the chief "invasionary" forces Yiddish has sent into the hallowed terrain of English. Much more significant, I think, is the adoption by English of linguistic *devices*, Yiddish in origin, to convey nuances of affection, compassion, displeasure, emphasis, disbelief, skepticism, ridicule, sarcasm, scorn. Examples abound:

1. Blithe dismissal via repetition with a *sh* play-on-the-first-sound: "Fat-shmat, as long as she's happy."
2. Mordant syntax: "Smart, he isn't."
3. Sarcasm via innocuous diction: "He only tried to shoot himself."

Perhaps the basic gesture of grievance and contempt in Yiddish is explained when "Isaac Bashevis Singer reminds us that Yiddish may be the only language on earth that has never been spoken by men in power."

> . . . Knowledge, among Jews, came to compensate for worldly rewards. Insight, I think, became a substitute for weapons:

one way to block the bully's wrath is to know him better than he knows himself.

Jews *had* to become psychologists, and their preoccupation with human, no less than divine, behavior made Yiddish remarkably rich in names for the delineation of character types. Little miracles of discriminatory precision are contained in the distinctions between such simpletons as a *nebech*, a *shlemiel*, a *shmendrick*, a *shnook*; or between such dolts as a *klutz*, a *yold*, a *Kuni Lemmel*, a *shlep*, a *Chaim Yankel*. All of them inhabit the kingdom of the ineffectual, but each is assigned a separate place in the roll call. The sense of differentiation is so acute in Yiddish that a word like, say, *paskudnyak* has no peer in any language I know for the vocal delineation of a nasty character. And Yiddish coins new names with ease for new personality types: A *nudnik* is a pest; a *phudnik* is a *nudnik* with a Ph.D.

Were I asked to characterize Yiddish—its style, its life story, its ambience—in one word, I would not hesitate: irrepressible. . . .

Few instruments of human speech have led so parlous a life, amidst such inhospitable neighbors, against such fierce opposition. And I know of no tongue so beset by schisms and fevers and ambivalences from within the community that had given it birth: Jews themselves.

HENDIADYS: CLICHÉ AS DOUBLE PROBE

Lead, kindly fowl! They always did: ask the ages. What bird has done yesterday man may do next year, be it fly, be it moult, be it hatch, be it agreement in the nest. For her socioscientific sense is sound as a bell, sir, her volucrine automutativeness right on normalcy: she knows, she just feels she was kind of born to lay and love eggs. . . .

—James Joyce, *Finnegans Wake*

108

L. P. Smith in *Words and Idioms* draws attention to a mysterious property of language, namely, the ineradicable power of doublets. The Greek word for these structures, *hendiadys* ("one through two"), draws attention to the Greek word for "word"—*mythos*. Doublets, by interface, create new forms of what James Hillman calls in *Emotion* "isomorphic unity." Phrases like "song and dance," "words and music" draw attention to the different senses and media that are encountered in doublets. It is one of Shakespeare's favorite figures: "The slings and arrows of outrageous fortune," "grunt and sweat," "to lie in cold obstruction and to rot," "here upon this bank and school of time." The popular use of the form can be noted in Freud and Jung, Gilbert and Sullivan, Wordsworth and Coleridge, Barnum and Bailey, Plato and Aristotle, art and life, sweetness and light, etc.

People seem to feel better satisfied with these expressions, as if they were handling brand names and commodities, even though they may know nothing whatever about the individuals or items— e.g., Dido and Aeneas, Paris and Helen, Tristan and Iseult.

Nobody has investigated why "moonlight and roses" is more

potent than "moonlight or roses." Why should "beer and skittles" persist as a powerful phrase when hardly anybody knows what "skittles" are? The gap or abrading interface between such components seems to resonate with great power in mind, as "pop and mom," "the one and the many," "the egg and I," "counter-anarchy," "the flesh and the devil."

These pairs may well depend upon both repetition and variation of components of sound. If the consonant doesn't repeat there is sometimes a counterpoint in the vowels or a marked cadence or harmony. Just as *oxymoron* is a small or compressed paradox, so this doublet form may be compressed myths. (Let us keep in mind *mythos*, a word.) Many perceptions may enter into the formation of a single word, and these doublets may be a useful way of observing the process of "word" formation: the word within the word unable to speak a word. Or is it like the sculpture lurking in the stone, waiting to be released by interface, by the shock of encounter with some other word or instrument? A much larger aspect of this same myth-making of isomorphic units is studied in *The King's Two Bodies* by Ernst Kantorowicz.

109

W. K. Wimsatt approaches the entire matter of dual vision and its attendant metamorphosis in *Hateful Contraries*:

> My view is that the English Augustans were, at their best and at their most characteristic, laughing poets of a heightened unreality. The world which the Augustan wit found most amusing and into which he had his deepest visions was an inverted, chaotic reality, the unreality of the "uncreating word,"—the "true No-meaning" which "puzzles more than Wit." The peculiar feat of the Augustan poet was the art of teasing unreality with the redeeming force of wit—of casting upon a welter of unreal materials a light of order and a perspective vision.
>
> That is the truth despite all the intimations to the contrary which Augustan poets themselves may have uttered, all the rules which later scholars may have identified, to the effect that Augustanism is the direct incorporation of ideal reality, of reason and light—"one clear, unchanged, and universal light."

Examples of Shakespeare's procedure in hendiadys readily illustrates how complex and witty the form can be: "To lie in cold obstruction and to rot" (*Measure for Measure*)—"obstruction" is itself a hendiadys of two latin words, *obstrudo* and *obstruo* (that are adjacent to one another in Cooper's *Thesaurus Linguae Romanae et Britannicae*, 1584, which work deeply repays the attention of any Shakespearean scholar.) Cooper says of *obstrudo*: "To rot: to drive a thing deep and hide it in the ground." Immediately below he gives *obstruo*: "To shut: to stop up: to make up a building: to hide another's prospect." Shakespeare's "To lie in cold obstruction" combines these in a hendiadys.

It is the same in Shakespeare's celebrated phrase in Macbeth: "Here upon this bank and school of time," which the editors have frequently amended to "Here upon this bank and shoal of time." The two environments that make up the hendiadys are inferred by the words "to trammel up" and "teach us bloody instructions." The hendiadys here trammels up two environments in one. The "bank" was Elizabethan for "school bench." (The trammel net itself is an interesting example of double-environment. It consists of two nets, one with fine and one with coarse holes. The fish pushes the fine net into one of the large holes of the coarse net.)

IDENTITY—THE CULTURE HERO

I go to encounter for the millionth time the reality of experience and to forge in the smithy of my soul the uncreated conscience of my race.

—James Joyce, *A Portrait of the Artist as a Young Man*

Love my label like myself.

—James Joyce, *Finnegans Wake*

(The lengthened shadow of a man

Is history, said Emerson

Who had not seen the silhouette

Of Sweeney straddled in the sun.)

—T. S. Eliot, "Sweeney Erect"

Philosophy from Aristotle onward had recognized the divine element within the human soul, the nature of which was more specifically defined by the Stoics: "For mortal to aid mortal—this is God, and this is the road to eternal glory." A noble formula, this, which Cicero develops: "Those men have within them a supernatural element and are destined for eternal life who regard themselves as born into the world to help and guard and preserve their fellow man. Hercules passed away to join the Gods: he would never so have passed unless in the course of his mortal life he had built for himself the road he traveled."

The antithesis of this image is that portrayed in *The Apes of God* by Wyndham Lewis—a group of parasites who are the apes of the apes of God. Lewis is prepared to concede that integral man is in some sense an "ape of God." "Apes," of course, is the Latin word for "bees," and the work of the bees is all sweetness and light. Thus, Lewis gets a good many levels of meaning into his title.

Dr. Johnson was prepared to view poets and artists as elevated beings, but he saw them very much as members of society. In *Rasselas*, when Imlac begins to rhapsodize about the poet, Johnson qualifies him:

> "He must write as the interpreter of nature, and the legislator of mankind, and consider himself as presiding over the thoughts and manner of future generations; as a being superior to time and place. . . ."
>
> Imlac now felt the enthusiastic fit, and was proceeding to aggrandize his own profession, when the prince cried out, "Enough! Thou has convinced me that no human being can ever be a poet."

113

What Imlac is restrained from uttering, Shelley uninhibitedly proclaimed in his "Defence of Poetry," echoing Johnson's phrase in his own assertion that poets are "the unacknowledged legislators of the world." In the Shelley context the poet is the "missing link" between heaven and earth; but in our own time it is the gap itself that has become the bond of being, as in quantum mechanics with its concept of resonance-as-bond.

Today, amidst the total involvement of living on a "scrapped" planet, everyone is encouraged to think of himself as a creative artist, divinely assigned to "do his thing." The culture hero undertakes to relate his world to reality by Herculean labors of probe and retrieval and purgation.

Edgar Friedenberg describes the adolescent quest for identity in our time:

> The process of becoming an American, as it goes on in high school, tends to be a process of renunciation of differences. This conflicts directly, of course, with the adolescent need for self-definition; but the conflict is so masked in in-

stitutionalized gaiety that the adolescent himself usually does not become aware of it. He must still deal with the alienation it engenders. . . .

In *War and Peace in the Global Village* the principal theme is the quest for identity through violence in a world of rapidly shifting technologies. A sudden change of environment through major technical innovations blurs the identity image of generations old and new. They then begin a tragic *agon* of redefinition of their image of identity.

Harold Rosenberg sees that in a period of speeded-up innovation there is a new kind of problem that concerns the scattering of existing arrangements fast enough to make room for the new ones:

> But the only vital tradition of twentieth-century art to which criticism can appeal is that of overthrowing tradition. This makes every attempt at criticism of contemporary art inherently comical. You get conservatives who want to overthrow the radical tradition; though if we got rid of this tradition, too, the result would be not as they imagine the recovery of some graver tradition but the absence of any tradition, mere confusion and anarchy, as we have seen in American ex-radicalism and in populist movements. In contrast to these anarchistic conservatives, you get traditionalist revolutionaries who, leaning back on the radical art of past decades, attack everything new on the ground that it does not come up to the revolutionary standard. Yet how can the radical artist be satisfied with the terminology of yesterday's revolts?
>
> "My aim," announces Sir Herbert, "has been to represent a consistently revolutionary attitude." This statement illustrates the comedy. Is it revolutionary to have a revolutionary attitude?

The task of the purgation of tradition is elaborated in the fifth labor of Heracles, the task of removing the dung from the folds, stables, and yards of King Augeias, son of Helios, the Sun-god. The dung had not been removed in a great while, and its environmental effects on the population of the Peloponnese had become unbearable. Heracles struck a bargain with Augeias that, in return for a tithe of the vast flocks and herds of the king, he would do the whole job in a day. The king gleefully envisaged Heracles immersed in a sea of dung, vainly bailing and bucketing and toting. Heracles merely proceeded to make gaps in the wall of the yard and diverted the adjacent rivers into these intervals. The rushing streams cleansed not only the yard and the stables but also the surrounding pastures and valleys.

When Mallarmé and Eliot and Pound and Joyce designate the poetic task as cleansing and renewal of speech and language, they point to an enterprise of even greater scope than that undertaken by Heracles. Language is be-fouled and messed up by millions of people each day. It is only periodically restored by poets who create new gaps or intervals in the central rhythms of the tongue. The fissures so opened admit and direct the streams of speech in fresh new patterns that release perceptual life from pestilential linguistic smog.

115

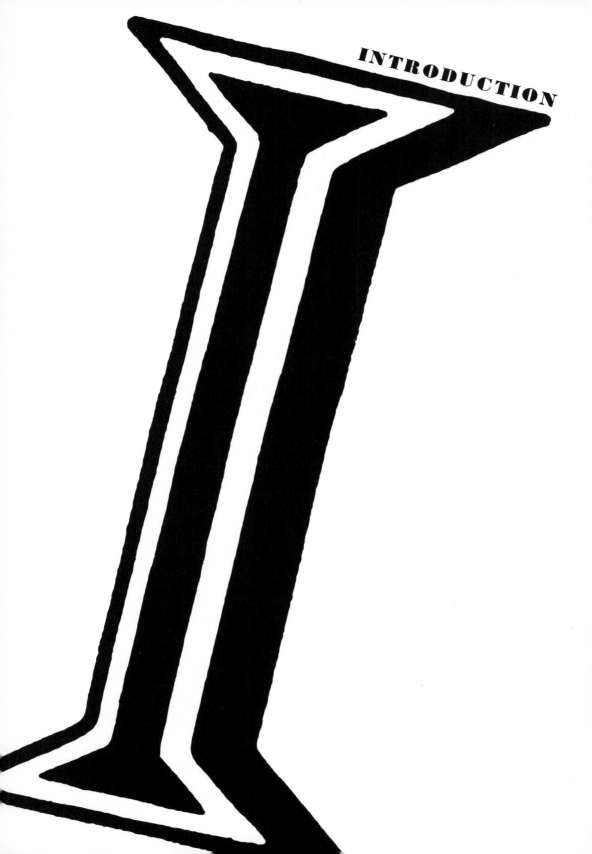

INTRODUCTION

Between the ancient and the modern worlds there has been a kind of reversal of roles for cliché and archetype. The inventor, the discoverer of new forms and new technologies, was for archaic man someone who was more than a man. "Surely some power more than human gave things their first names," says Socrates in the *Phaedrus*. A modern Eskimo said to Professor E. S. Carpenter, "How could I know stone if there were no word 'stone'?" To archaic man language is an immediate evoker of reality, a magical form. In the same way, he thinks of the "apple of his eye" as constituting his visual world, not as receiving it.

The idea of words as merely corresponding to reality, the idea of matching, is characteristic only of highly literal cultures in which the visual sense is dominant. Today in the age of quantum mechanics, for which the "chemical bond" is, according to Heisenberg and Linus Pauling and others, a "resonance," it is perfectly natural to resume a "magical" attitude to language. The poetry of statement became the crux of one of the great critical upheavals of the twentieth century. This change corresponds to the discovery that consciousness is also a multileveled event with its roots in the "deepest terrors and desires."

It might be argued that a main cause of the merging of the archaic attitude to cliché with the modern notion of archetype as a more intense reality resulted from our great variety of new techniques of retrieval. Both past cultures and primal individual experiences are now subject to ready and speedy access. The ancient world had fewer means and fewer motives for retrieving the past just in the degree to which it considered all past events as present. The medieval need for the retrieval of ancient Greek and Latin and Hebrew for scriptural study began a cult of historical scholarship under modest conditions of manuscript culture. Today the means of retrieval of historical cultures and events is so extensive that it involves our time in depth in ancient cults and mysteries.

As we meditate upon the ancient clichés or sacro-breakthroughs, the literal man is inclined to consider them as "archetypes." For example, Northrop Frye in *Anatomy of Criticism* defines archetype as "a symbol, usually an image, which recurs often enough in literature to be recognizable as an element of one's literary experience as a whole." Of course this particular definition is most un-Jungian in suggesting that archetypes are human artifacts produced by much repetition—in other words, a form of cliché. For the literary archetypalist there is always a problem of whether *Oedipus Rex* or *Tom Jones* would have the same effect on an audience in the South Sea Islands as in Toronto. With the new means of plenary cultural retrieval, ancient clichés are taking their place as transcendental or archetypal forms.

This raises a central matter that will be discussed more fully. It is the process by which new clichés or new technological probes and environments have the effect of liquidating or scrapping the preceding clichés of cultures and environments created by preceding technologies. The world of archaeology and musicology today is entirely concerned with classifying these rejected fragments of obsolete and broken cultures. It is in "The Circus Animals' Desertion" that Yeats reviews this whole process, which was inherent in his entire creative procedure, as can be seen in "Leda and the Swan."

If we can consider form the reversing of archetype into cliché, as for example, the use of an archetypal Ulysses in James Joyce's novel to explore contemporary consciousness in the city of Dublin, then we may ask what would be the status of this pattern in primordial times, in the medieval period, and today. The answer would seem to be that in primordial times and today this archetype-into-cliché process is perfectly normal and accepted but that in the medieval period it is exceptional and unusual. The Balinese say, "We have no art, we do everything as well as possible." The artist in the Middle Ages, Renaissance, or the era up to the nineteenth century was regarded as a unique, exceptional person because he used an exceptional, unusual process. In primordial times,

as today, the artist uses a familiar, ordinary technique and so he
is looked upon as an ordinary, familiar person. Every man today
is in this sense an artist—the administrator, the scientist, the doctor,
as well as the man who uses paint or sculpts stone. Just as the
archaic man had to follow natural processes of rhythms in order to
influence and to purge, cleanse them by *ricorso*, so modern electric
technologies require such timing and precision that only the following of processes in nature can be tolerated. The immediately preceding centuries of mechanization had been able to bypass these
processes by fragmentation and strip-mining kinds of procedures.
The very word "cliché" derives from the mechanical processes of
printing, as we have noted. The Gutenberg technology of imposing
and impressing by means of fragmented and repeatable units was
the cue for all succeeding mechanization of the social and educational and political establishments. As various technologies have
succeeded print, it has become more and more the home of the
archetype.

Any breakthrough, whether for the poet or for the engineer, such   119
as Daedalus or Hermes or Prometheus, seemed to reverberate with
the divine thunder. The ceaseless use and repetition of these dis-
coverers was sacralized. Eliade, in *Cosmos and History*, states:

> In the particulars of his conscious behavior, the "primi-
> tive," the archaic man, acknowledges no act which has not
> been previously posited and lived by someone else, some other
> being who was not a man. What he does has been done before.
> His life is the ceaseless repetition of gestures initiated by
> others.

For archaic or tribal man there was no past, no history. Always
present. Today we experience a return to that outlook when technological breakthroughs have become so massive as to create one
environment upon another, from telegraph to radio to TV to satellite. These forms give us instant access to all pasts. As for tribal
man, there is for us no history. All is present, including the tribal
man studied by Eliade.

The assumption of cliché as a breakthrough, as a probe into
a new dimension, is challenged by Plato. His cave is the first "rag-

and-bone shop," to use Yeats's phrase, the first archetypal store-house. The sacralizing of the archetype was the work of civilized man with his literate, historical perspective. Petrarch, "the first modern man," stood on the border between two worlds, as one student put it: "With one foot firmly planted in the Middle Ages, while with the other he saluted the rising star of the Renaissance." His *Ruins of Rome* began the humanist cult of the rag-and-bone shop. The very small part of antiquity accessible to the twelfth-century historian was brought to bear upon the task of the exegesis of scripture. The sacralizing of the archetype, or ancient form, was not characteristic of the pagan world. For that world the words of Eliade describe the role of the archetype:

> What does living mean for a man who belongs to a tradi-
> tional culture? Above all, it means living in accordance with
> extrahuman models, in conformity with archetypes. Hence it
> means living at the heart of the *real* since . . . there is nothing
> truly real except the archetypes. Living in conformity with
> the archetypes amounted to respecting the "law," since the
> law was only a primordial hierophany, the revelation *in illo*
> *tempore* of the norms of existence, a disclosure by a divinity
> or a mystical being. And if, through the repetition of para-
> digmatic gestures and by means of periodic ceremonies,
> archaic man succeeded, as we have seen, in annulling time,
> he none the less lived in harmony with the cosmic rhythms;
> we could even say that he entered into these rhythms (we need
> only remember how "real" night and day are to him, and the
> seasons, the cycles of the moon, the solstices).

Naturally, the Old Testament repudiated this archetypal world as understood by pagan man. It repudiated all technologies as pagan deities, from the Tower of Babel to the Golden Calf. For Christian culture the scrapping or superannuation of the formulas and rituals and technologies sacred to pagan man became a natural form of behavior; but the door was now wide open for technological innovation in a merely humanist context. Christian contempt for the world and its works has had much to do with shaping attitudes toward cliché and formulaic models of organizing experience. In the same way Christian indifference to the "supernatural" claims of human invention and arts of the Muses encouraged meditation on the world as a vast ruin. Paradoxically, it was this indifference to the traditional that permitted novelty and innovation to thrive unhindered by religious observations. A single book serves to illuminate this entire theme: Lynn White's *Medieval Technology and Social Change* is an account of a wide range of technical inventions unknown to archaic man. Such inventions as the horse collar quickly led to the development of the modern world. Archaic man, as presented to us by Eliade and a host of contemporary anthropologists, had a huge stake in fixity and in an unchanging order, like the French Academy scrutinizing neologisms. Stasis is a strange facet of tribal and oral cultures, as revealed in *The Lore and Language of School Children* by Iona and Peter Opie.

Christian indifference to the pagan rituals of stability and renewal, as well as Christian contempt for the world as a wreck or middenheap, tended to reverse the pattern of cliché and archetype that characterized prehistoric man. This reversal stands out clearly today when we experience a return to the prehistoric attitudes to both cliché and archetype. Our technological breakthroughs are on a superior human scale, re-creating total new environments, greatly enlarging the Emperor's wardrobe, and making possible a reprograming of the totality of existence on the planet. It is these developments that have restored cliché-as-probe and put invention in a position of dominance over the archetype.

121

Since we have already raised the theme of printing as related to cliché and archetype, the complexities of this innovation can be seen in *Finnegans Wake*, where Joyce is not only discussing the subject but illustrating the linguistic means for tackling it on several levels at once (see page 122).

Line 1 indicates that the process of creating a cliché for use or probe begins in taking something petite or pretty as a means of extending its action to include the *holos*. This is cliché in its sacro-archaic character and it is also cliché in the sense of dull habituation. The *part* may be a tooth. In a sense, teeth are not only the feature of the animal body where repetition and lineality concur, but when followed by "an allforabit" (alphabet) as their issue, recall the fable of King Cadmus and "the dragon's teeth which

1 When a part so ptee does duty for the holos we soon grow to use of an
2 allforabit. Here (please to stoop) are selveran cued peteet peas of
3 quite a pecuniar interest inaslittle as they are the pellets that make
4 the tomtummy's pay roll. Right rank ragnar rocks and with these
5 rox orangotangos rangled rough and rightgorong. Wisha, wisha,
6 whydidtha? Thik is for thorn that's thuck in its thoil like thum-
7 fool's thraitor thrust for vengeance. What a mnice old mness it
8 all mnakes! A middenhide hoard of objects! Olives, beets, kim-
9 mells, dollies, alfrids, beatties, cormacks and daltons. Owlets' eegs
10 (O stoop to please!) are here, creakish from age and all now
11 quite epsilene, and oldwolldy ·wobblewers, haudworth a wipe o
12 grass. Sss! See the snake wurrums everyside! Our durlbin is
13 sworming in sneaks. They came to our island from triangular
14 Toucheaterre beyond the wet prairie rared up in the midst of the
15 cargon of prohibitive pomefructs but along landed Paddy Wip-
16 pingham and the his garbagecans cotched the creeps of them
17 pricker than our whosethere outofman could quick up her whats-
18 thats. Somedivide and sumthelot but the tally turns round the
19 same balifuson. Racketeers and bottloggers.
20   Axe on thwacks on thracks, axenwise. One by one place one
21 be three dittoh and one before. Two nursus one make a plaus-
22 ible free and idim behind. Starting off with a big boaboa and three-
23 legged calvers and ivargraine jadesses with a message in their
24 mouths. And a hundreadfilled unleavenweight of liberorumqueue
25 to con an we can till allhorrors eve. What a meanderthalltale to
26 unfurl and with what an end in view of squattor and anntisquattor
27 and postproneauntisquattor! To say too us to be every tim, nick
28 and larry of us, sons of the sod, sons, littlesons, yea and lealittle-
29 sons, when usses not to be, every sue, siss and sally of us, dugters
30 of Nan! Accusative ahnsire! Damadam to infinities!
31.   True there was in nillohs dieybos as yet no lumpend papeer
32 in the waste and mightmountain Penn still groaned for the micies
33 to let flee. All was of anciented. You gave me a boot (signs on
34 it!) and I ate the wind. I quizzed you a quid (with for what?) and
35 you went to the quod. But the world, mind, is, was and will be
36 writing its own wrunes for ever, man, on all matters that fall
37 under the ban of our infrarational senses . . .

THIS IS
A PRINTING OFFICE

CROSSROADS OF CIVILIZATION
REFUGE OF ALL THE ARTS
AGAINST THE RAVAGES OF TIME
ARMOURY OF FEARLESS TRUTH
AGAINST WHISPERING RUMOUR
INCESSANT TRUMPET OF TRADE

FROM THIS PLACE WORDS MAY
FLY ABROAD
NOT TO PERISH ON WAVES OF SOUND
NOT TO VARY WITH THE
WRITER'S HAND
BUT FIXED IN TIME HAVING BEEN
VERIFIED IN PROOF

FRIEND YOU STAND ON
SACRED GROUND

THIS IS A PRINTING OFFICE

123

sprang up armed men." The letters of the alphabet in their early mode were pictograms that offered many relationships to the *holos*, as the famous phrase "alpha and the plough." Letters permitted specialism in human organization, which is inseparable from the military life. It also creates a social order or hierarchy (as in line 2—"please to stoop"). The use of an alphabet is a great drop in dignity from the full magical power of the spoken word in archaic ritual. It is "stooping to conquer," in many senses. "Stoop" is "step" and in cliché technology a step that can be up or down. It is a means of control and power. Joyce is saying that no cliché or technology can be accepted without great loss to the integral being of the *holos*, and proceeds to a witty evocation of the psychic and social consequences of the "allforabit" beginning with the effect on human identity.

"Selveran" (line 2) resonates with the modalities of the individual self in relation to the little module bits ("peteet peas"). Throughout the *Wake* the theme of the mass-man, whether preliterate or postliterate, is alluded to many times via the "mush of porter pease." The condition of the self as merged in tribe or society is like that of the individual pea mashed. It is the mashing, of course, that creates (line 4) the pay roll. Money, as repetitive module, is only one of the many side effects of the allforabit. "Tomtummy's" (line 4) recalls that an army of Tommies not only marches on its tummy, but is roused by the roll of drums and tom-toms. "Wisha, wisha" (line 5) introduces the driving emotion in in all technological cliché development. It is alluded to under many forms in the *Wake*: "a burning would is come to dance inane," and of course, "the willingdone musiroom"—a massive collection of human cliché and weaponry by which "a burning would" manifests itself in ever new environments and power.

"Wisha, wisha" alludes also to another theme that goes with "peteet peas" (line 2), namely "mishe, mishe," the Celtic for "I am" and the tribal mishe of the wild Irish, or "a mush and a wish."

The query (line 6) "Whydidtha?" follows the chain of consequences resulting from a single bit, or bite (line 2) "allforabit." The "a" is for "apple," as it were. The image of the "thorn that's thuck in its thoil" (line 6) is one of the punishments for the bite—

his toil in the garden that has now become a mess. The word "mness" (line 7) mimes the mouth full of apple, as it were. "A middenhide hoard of objects" (line 8) recalls the impulse of fallen man to cover himself (hides, skins). Instead of plucking the fruit as it grows, he now specializes in the production of the hoard of objects and a diversity of diets. Man becomes a producer and a consumer, organizing trade and markets with ensuing wars ("cormacks and daltons" [line 9] . . . "Racketeers and bottloggers" [line 19]). It's the money economy, i.e. "allforabit" where "the tally turns round the same balifuson" (lines 18-19).

The entire page is devoted to tracing the "meanderthalltale" (line 25), the labyrinthine ways of the alphabet technology as a kind of prototype of all cliché or breakthroughs. One of the principal effects of "allforabit" specialism is not only the production of a "hoard of objects" (line 8) but the endless tossing of same onto the middenheap. New technology as an automatic means of scrapping or rejecting the preceding culture creates the "liberorumqueue" (line 24), the endless production "to con an we can" (line 25).

Writing as a means of retrieving "ancientry" (line 33) led to a vast scrap heap of retrieved data even before the advent of "lumpend paper" (line 31). The middenhide grows mountainous with the castoffs of cultures and technologies. One theme in "middenhide" is the popular invisible quality of the environments created by new cliché or techniques. The forms of these technologies are imprinted not only on human language but on the outer world as well: "But the world, mind, is, was and will be writing its own wrunes for ever, man, on all matters" (lines 35-36) gave us the "ruins," the deciphering and retrieval of which fascinates the literate humanist.

Vico, in his *Scienza Nuova*, which Joyce found so useful, stresses that all ancient fables and tales are really records of moments of technical breakthrough to which the ancients assigned the status and name of a god, but Vico also insisted that the effects of such breakthroughs were recorded in the new "wrunes" (line 36), writing into the patterns of human speech and sensibility. Vico, like Joyce, insists that new technology is not added to culture, but it "ruins" whole societies, tossing them onto the middenhide or heap, whence they are forever being retrieved and refurbished by succeeding generations.

This page of the *Wake*, like many others, is an approach to Yeats's "rag-and-bone shop of the heart." It is the tradition from which the individual talent must filch the fragments that he will shore against his own ruins. For Joyce, as for Yeats, the rag-and-bone shop is a collection of abandoned clichés.

It is the clichés that are the invented probes of artists and society, enabling them to ascend or descend the ladder of human accomplishment: "please to stoop" (line 2) and "O stoop to please" (line 10). The need of the poet for ever-new means of probing and exploration of experience sends him back again and again to the rag-and-bone shop of abandoned cliché. The testimony of artists in this matter is impressive. The stages by which the literary archetype became substituted for the technical cliché as the means of creation is one of the subjects of this book.

126   As a case in point, Yeats begins "The Circus Animals' Desertion" by saying:

> I sought a theme and sought for it in vain,
> I sought it daily for six weeks or so.
> Maybe at last, being but a broken man,
> I must be satisfied with my heart, although
> Winter and summer till old age began
> My circus animals were all on show,
> Those stilted boys, that burnished chariot,
> Lion and woman and the Lord knows what.

This poem is a *ricorso* or rehearsal, a retrieval of Yeats's entire career. Seeing himself as an old man, he has thrown himself on the scrap heap. He has archetypalized himself, but first he rehearses all the clichés of his art, all the innovations that he had introduced into the drama and poetry of his time.

> What can I but enumerate old themes?

Having surveyed these stages of his art, his innovations and experiments, he simply says,

> Those masterful images because complete,
> Grew in pure mind, but out of what began?

His answer presents the main theme of *From Cliché to Archetype*:
the new poetic techniques and images are retrieved from

> A mound of refuse or the sweepings of a street,
> Old kettles, old bottles, and a broken can,
> Old iron, old bones, old rags, that raving slut
> Who keeps the till. . . .

Yeats brings in here the whole theme of commerce as part of the
poetic process. His poetic exhibitionism onto the big top is done.
The images retrieved from "the rag-and-bone shop" out of which
he built his ladder for the high-wire act are now complete and cast
aside. His "Jacob's ladder" is gone.

"I must lie down where all the ladders start." Our theme in
From Cliché to Archetype is simply the scrapping of all poetic
innovation and cliché when it has reached a certain stage of use.
Masterful forms and images, when complete, are cast aside to
become "the rag-and-bone shop of the heart"—that is, the world
of the archetype.

127

What about Jacob's ladder? Jacob lay down only to climb a
ladder, or to dream, at least, of a ladder of angels ascending and
descending in heavenly hierarchy. Yeats regards the moment of
poetic breakdown as a new breakthrough, the beginning again of
the ascent and descent of Jacob's ladder of heavenly vision.

As his poetic clichés collapse and are scrapped, he turns to the
retrieval of old forms for new clichés. It is the worn-out cliché that
reveals the creative or archetypal processes in language as in all
other processes and artifacts.

J. Seznec in *The Survival of the Pagan Gods* provides an entire
study of the process of desacralization of the gods by literary
humanism from the third century B.C. to the Renaissance. The
process consisted in accepting the gods as technology heroes, or
geniuses, who devoted their lives to the good of their fellow men.
The recognition of the human element in the gods tended at first
to be used against them, but beginning with Isadore of Seville's
Etymologiae, a seventh-century encyclopedia, authors had begun

to accept a desacralized view of the gods. The new strategy was followed throughout the Middle Ages and until the *Scienza Nuova* of Giambattista Vico. Like Isadore of Seville, Vico saw the history of cultural evolution in the etymologies of words as recording responses to technological innovations.

The encyclopedic tradition of classical rhetoric accepted the gods on a multi-leveled exegesis basis. This "grammatical" method of literary analysis via the figurative, tropological (moral), and anagogical (high mysteries) retained the old tribal and magical tradition of the "gods" approach by literary techniques of retrieval. It follows that the sixteenth- and seventeenth-century Puritans, in rejecting the multi-leveled literary approach also rejected the pagan "gods." The insistence on the single level of literal interpretation is the one that led Milton to toss the whole caboodle of pagan deities into his Hell, just as Plato had tossed all the multi-leveled phenomena of the world into his cave.

There may be something odd about the Paleolithic cave culture being dismissed by Plato into a Spenserian Cave of Error. But just as the plenary retrieval techniques of Gutenberg print created the Puritan ideal of a recovery of a purified and primitive Christianity, so the modern anthropologist, using plenary methods of retrieval, has rejected the traditional humanistic or literary view of the gods in favor of a complete resacralizing of pagan art and ritual. The resacralizing of the ancient clichés of ancient technology by anthropologists places the literary archetypalist in a very embarrassing position. The archetypalist, having come to regard the gods as a neutered or "spayed" bunch of moralized entities, now confronts the anthropologist, who insists on accepting them as real wild environmental forces completely beyond literary occurrence or control. The gods as cliché technologies are not susceptible to literary classification.

W. K. Wimsatt in "Horses of Wrath" details the conventional procedure of the literary man when he turns to the *Anatomy of Criticism* by Northrop Frye:

> Some of the ideas of the arch-mythopoeist of our time have been foreshadowed, in fact appropriated, in the preceding

paragraph. Northrop Frye's *Fearful Symmetry* (1949) announced in the last chapter the Blakean inspiration of an apocalyptic construct which came to realization in his Four Essays entitled *Anatomy of Criticism* (1957). Earlier drafts and later applications are collected in his *Fables of Identity* (1963). The *Anatomy*, especially in its "Polemical Introduction," is written from an exceedingly keen awareness of the history of criticism and of the problems for criticism which we have just been surveying. It intends to escape from the main problem of criticism—that of literary evaluation—by the announcement of a very bold separation—that is, simply a separation of the act of "criticizing" literature from the act of valuing it.

This is something like what both Eliot and Richards at moments in their thought during the 1920's had touched upon, but it now appears with a surpassing starkness and insistence. I refrain from saying "with systematic insistence," because, although the whole volume is an astonishing invention, I believe that the confrontation of the concepts of value and criticism is never in fact squarely made, and not only that the Four Essays themselves are in fact heavily charged with value assertions and implications, but that the Polemical Introduction, where the main argument about value is carried on, is notable for a series of finely disguised contradictions in this respect.

Homer's Ulysses descended into Hell to consult the ancients, oracle-style (cf. Eliot's "Tradition and the Individual Talent"). Plato, with the help of the new technological cliché of the written word, tossed the whole world of becoming into the middenhide of his cave. Virgil's Book VI is in the Homeric tradition of consulting the wisdom of the tribe.

Dante's Hell, complete with a few celebrated historical figures, is a sort of social register of his society. His Hell is a minutely discriminating structure of psychological states. Critics have commented upon the grandeur of the vagueness of Milton's Hell in comparison with the concretely imagined Hell of Dante. Considered as a scrap heap of rejected pagan technologies or clichés, Milton's Hell is amazingly specific, cataloguing a great many of the pagan deities and characterizing them with revelatory attributes. It is not difficult to see how Milton has junked the entire pagan cultures, even what to him must have been the attractive technologies of eloquence and poetry and speculative philosophy. Even his favorite art, music, is dispensed with for its technological seductiveness.

In *Paradise Lost* we have a later and fuller version of the youthful Milton's "On the Morning of Christ's Nativity," in which Milton sees the infant Christ almost like a new technology, superannuating the pagan ones. Whereas the pagans' hells omitted the gods of the technologies and of the arts, Milton's Hell receives all the whole company and seems almost to be designed for that purpose. Dante's Hell is a place of physical and psychological torment, but Milton's Hell is an Apollonian museum of pagan antiquity and of the arts and senses.

There is a sort of parallel between the world of Plato's cave as the recipient of a rejected world, where Plato had been replaced by Euclidean rational space and the Socratic probe (derivative from the new cliché of the written word) and the world of the seventeenth century, where Gutenberg print played the role of the earlier phonetic script. The seventeenth-century mechanist tossed aside the whole human past, relegating it to Milton's Hell.

To wanton with the Sun her lusty Paramour.

. . . . . .

   She crown'd with Olive green, came softly sliding
Down through the turning sphear
His ready Harbinger,
   With Turtle wing the amorous clouds dividing,
And waving wide her mirtle wand,
She strikes a universall Peace through Sea and Land.

—John Milton, "On the Morning of Christ's Nativity"

130

JOKES

"Funferall at Finnegans Wake"

It is naturally incongruous that a funeral could be an occasion of merriment. Have with you to the anthropologists if you want to know further details. This is a universal custom to fend off all ill forces and events attending death. Thus, the whole of the *Wake* is a kind of jig. And so it is with Lawrence Sterne's *Tristram Shandy*. Of Sterne, Joyce said he should have been called Swift, and Swift should have been called Sterne. The swift is a bird, a martin, and if the wit of Swift was grim ("Satire is a sort of glass, wherein beholders do generally discover everybody's face but their own"), the Sterne touch was light.

Sterne's hero, Tristram Shandy, was buoyant and swift in his motions. The whole erudite game that he plays throughout is ostensibly the expiation of a grievance against the ignoble circumstances in which he was named "Tristram." Sterne also perpetrates a huge spoof on the history of the printing press, parodying both the processes of print and publishing, and their consequences in destroying classical eloquence. The stages from Isocrates to James Joyce, by which eloquence and wisdom alike were achieved by erudition, are a principal subject of paradox in Erasmus, and Swift, and Sterne and Joyce.

The man who said there are only five basic forms of joke was obviously unaware of the *Wake*. "Laughter," said Wyndham Lewis, "is an explosion of nervous energy attacking the muscles of the face." In every sense it is thus a cultural and psychological interface. It is inevitable that the funny man be "a man with a grievance," as Steve Allen reminds us in *The Funny Men*. The mere names of Twain and Leacock and Chaplin serve to recall their bitterness. Social anger and sensitivity sharpen the awareness of the funny man so that his "jokes" are stabs or probes into the cultural matrix that plagues him.

Conversely, anyone can determine an area of social irritation and disturbance by simply checking the areas from which jokes are currently emerging. The probes or jokes generated in one area are frequently transferred for service to new areas. The "Polack" or Italian jokes are at present current in Canada as "Newfie jokes." The Newfoundland population has shifted very recently. The coast-dwellers have been transferring to the towns, with resulting new confrontations. When grievances or irritations become too severe, the joke ceases to function as a catharsis. The north of Ireland has not been supplying much humor lately, and the stock of Vietnam jokes is small.

The Eskimo brings the trader a copy of the *Manhattan* and says, "I carve what I see."

The funny man as a professional clown puts on the corporate mask of a collective grievance. Jack Benny's stingy grimace and W. C. Fields' choleric profile serve to siphon off great stores of collective irritation and frustration in a society.

At another level, every emperor must have his clown, or "licensed fool." In rigid hierarchical societies only this licensed character dare exercise the probe of free speech. The clown is indispensable as audience-tester and as checker on the moods of the ruling figure. Again, without his clown, the emperor has no means of contact with the public.

133

Sigmund Freud uses Jewish marriage-broker jokes to illustrate the interplay of different areas of experience in his title *Wit and Its Relation to the Unconscious.*

The Joys of Yiddish by Leo Rosten is an encyclopedia of humor as minority grievance and insight: "Knowledge, among Jews, came to compensate for worldly rewards. Insight, I think, became a substitute for weapons: one way to block the bully's wrath is to know him better than he knows himself."

But Sterne knew that knowledge is the "supreme bully" and that the only way to get on equal terms with Socrates is to exercise the intercostal muscles with laughter. Like prayer, it is "getting born backwards," as the holy sister explains in a recent play. It is Oedipus getting unfaked.

LOVEJOY AND THE DAISY CHAIN

Those aren't love beads, they're flea collars!

ARMSTRONG to ALDRIN: "What are those colored beads on the window?"
ALDRIN: "That's the constellation Urina."

News item: Russian biologist links glow-worms with body lice, enabling whole populations to read *Pravda* in bed.

I want to hold your hand.
> —The Beatles

Mitt me Mutt.

The handshake was the gesture of undying enmity in archaic societies. (See Herbert Spencer's studies.)

> Simple and faithless as the shake of a hand.
> > —Laforgue

> Shake hands and come out fighting.

> It's better to have loved and lost than never to have lost at all.
> > —Samuel Butler

Without the great chain of being there would have been no "missing link." The flower people, making daisy chains, are the missing links, or gaps and interfaces between the old industrial and new electric cultures.

> We've squared the circle, but you can't square a daisy
> chain with its broken chromosomes.
>
> —Flower-people saying

In every tongue there is a phrase that indicates the feeling of complete knowledge or mastery of some matter while indicating the sensory bias of the whole culture. In English we may say, "I know it like the back of my hand" (visual?). In Russian they say, "I know it like the palm of my hand" (iconic tactile?). In Spanish they say, "I know it as if I had given birth to it" (proprioceptive-visceral?). The Americans say, "I know it inside out" (kinetic-manipulatory?). The Thailanders say, "I know it like a snake swimming in water" (the dance of thought among words?). In German they say, "I know it like the inside of my pocket" (tactile-interface?). In French they say, "I know it *au fond*" (auditory-resonant?). The Japanese, masters of touch or interval, say, "I know it from head to toe."

Perhaps when we say, "I have it on the tip of my tongue," we mean that word or phrase is teetering between visual and audible recall. When we say, "I have it at my fingertips," we indicate an immediacy and profundity of access.

In mimicking the sound of a dog, the Japanese say, "Wung wung"; the Polish say, "Peef peef"; and the Americans say, "Bow wow." The "plot slickens" as we turn to the immediate extensions of our senses.

Joyce sets up the chain of cognition and recognition itself:

> In the ignorance that implies impression that knits knowledge that finds the nameform that whets the wits that convey contacts that sweeten sensation that drives desire that adheres to attachment that dogs death that bitches birth that entails the ensuance of existentiality.

Rowan and Martin's Laugh-In's Lily Tomlin follows this path. No one has to make sense out of Goldie Hawn. Goldie (to Jack Benny): "Don't read the idiot card, just keep it going."

MATCHING SENSE

My object all sublime

I shall achieve in time,

To let the punishment fit the crime,

The punishment fit the crime;

And make each prisoner pent

Unwilling represent

A source of innocent merriment,

Of innocent merriment.

—W. S. Gilbert, *The Mikado*

Why then Ile fit you. Hieronymo's mad againe.
—T. S. Eliot, *The Waste Land*

However, we must not trust to the analogy with vision to further the theory of hearing.
—Edwin G. Boring, *The Physical Dimensions of Consciousness*

What Happened to the American Dream?
Or, The 7 Pillows of Was-dom

Daniel Boorstin's *The Image, or What Happened to the American Dream* is an interesting documentation of the somnambulist literary demand for matching as a criterion of integrity. Professor Boorstin enumerates fascinating examples of how new cliché technologies scrap the various features of the old American dream: "That's a fine child you have there, M'am." "That's nothing, wait until you see his photograph." The same "pseudo-event" pattern Professor Boorstin finds in all areas of American life, from news and entertainment to travel and politics. With the coming of film and TV, representative government itself has been transformed into image-making, a subculture of Madison Avenue PR. The American dream that has been scrapped is, of course, that of "the open road," which has now merged with jet city.

E. R. Leach, in his study of the *Politcal Systems of Highland Burma*, illustrates the futility of seeking for a literary consistency and matching, among myths:

> Now, in the past, Kachin ethnographers have never appreciated this point. They have regarded tradition as a species of badly recorded history. Where they have found inconsistencies in the record, they have felt justified in selecting that version which seemed most likely to be "true" or even in inventing parts of the story which appeared to be missing.
>
> Such an approach to the data makes it possible to represent the basic structure of Kachin society as very simple. Confusions of practice are regarded as due to the fact that the stupid Kachins fail to understand their own society or to obey their own rules. Enriquez, for example, has reduced the whole structural system to a couple of paragraphs.

139

Charles Moorman, in his *Arthurian Triptych*, adopts a mythic approach somewhat similar to that of E. R. Leach:

> It is apparent that all the defects of these possible ways of looking at myth in literature can be reduced to one fault. Myth is currently used as a sort of universal literary solvent; the unspoken assumption would seem to be "Let us reduce this poem, this novel, this play to its basic mythical, structural, ritual ingredients and there will then be an end to all critical problems."

In 1923, T. S. Eliot contributed to *The Dial* his essay on *"Ulysses, Order and Myth."*

It is here that Mr. Joyce's parallel use of the *Odyssey* has a great importance. It has the importance of a scientific discovery. No one else has built a novel upon such a foundation before: it has never before been necessary. I am not begging the question in calling *Ulysses* a "novel"; and if you call it an epic it will not matter. If it is not a novel, that is simply because the novel is a form which will no longer serve; it is because the novel, instead of being a form, was simply the expression of an age which had not sufficiently lost all form to feel the need of something stricter. Mr. Joyce has written one novel—*The Portrait*; Mr. Wyndham Lewis has written one novel—*Tarr*. I do not suppose that either of them will ever write another "novel." The novel ended with Flaubert and with James. It is, I think, because Mr. Joyce and Mr. Lewis, being "in advance" of their time, felt a conscious or probably unconscious dissatisfaction with the form, that their novels are more formless than those of a dozen clever writers who are unaware of its obsolescence.

In using the myth, in manipulating a continuous parallel between contemporaneity and antiquity, Mr. Joyce is pursuing a method which others must pursue after him. They will not be imitators, any more than the scientist who uses the discoveries of an Einstein in pursuing his own, independent, further investigations. It is simply a way of controlling, of ordering, of giving a shape and a significance to the immense panorama of futility and anarchy which is contemporary history. It is a method already adumbrated by Mr. Yeats, and of the need for which I believe Mr. Yeats to have been the first contemporary to be conscious. It is a method for which the horoscope is auspicious. Psychology (such as it is, and whether our reaction to it be comic or serious), ethnology, and *The Golden Bough* have concurred to make possible what was impossible even a few years ago. Instead of narrative method, we may now use the mythical method. It is, I seriously believe, a step toward making the modern world possible for art, toward that order and form which Mr. Aldington so earnestly desires. And only those who have won their own discipline in secret and without aid, in a world which offers

very little assistance to that end, can be of any use in further-
ing this advance.

Mr. Eliot is quite explicit about myth as a structure of parallels
without connectives. Mythic form is necessarily double. Its doubleness is a matter not of matching but of making, not of the mirror
and reflection but of the lamp and illumination. A great mass of
misconceptions has grown up around myth in the literary mind,
for it is natural to literary people to look for matching as a criterion of truth even in science. Introducing his book *Political
Systems of Highland Burma*, E. R. Leach writes:

> Differences of culture are, I admit, structurally significant,
> but the mere fact that two groups of people are of different
> culture does not necessarily imply—as has nearly always been
> assumed—that they belong to two quite different social sys-
> tems. In this book I assume the contrary.

Leach took great pains to correct a misplaced and irrelevant attempt at "mirroring" that pervades not only anthropological but
also literary thinking:

> I think it is fair to say that most British social anthropolo-
> gists commonly look upon myth from much the same point
> of view as that adopted by Malinowski in his well-known
> essay *Myth in Primitive Psychology*. According to this view
> myth and tradition are to be thought of primarily as a sanc-
> tion or charter for ritual action. Ritual action reflects the so-
> cial structure, but it is also a dramatic recapitulation of the
> myth....

James Joyce carries similar insights much further by relating myth
and ritual to the process of sensory cognition:

> *I pick up your reproof, the horsegift of a friend,*
> *For the prize of your save is the price of my spend.*
> *Can castwhores pulladeftkiss if oldpollocks forsake 'em*
> *Or Culex feel etchy if Pulex don't wake him?*
> *A locus to loue, a term it t'embarass,*
> *These twain are the twins that tick* Homo Vulgaris.

Joyce is carefully analyzing the nature of the cognitive process as extended in our technologies. Each extension creates a new environment that inflicts change and new motivation upon the old one. The old and the new environment are "twins" that perpetually impel us onward in a nonstop process of transformation. Joyce and Eliot and Pound never ceased to stress the importance of this complementary matching process for the understanding of poetry and human experience.

The reader of *The Mirror and the Lamp* can easily adapt W. H. Abrams' fine chapter on "Changing Metaphors of Mind" to the complementary roles of cliché and archetype. Abrams shows how richly Wordsworth and Coleridge contributed to the interplay of mind and external Nature:

> Which do both give it being and maintain
> A balance, an ennobling interchange
> Of action from without and from within;
> The excellence, pure function, and best power
> Both of the object seen, and eye that sees.

142

As the industrial environment formed new cliché-probes, poets and artists alike agreed to retrieve the old agrarian environment as archetypal forms. It was Petrarch and *The Ruins of Rome* once more. The agricultural and handicraft world of the pre-industrial technology quickly became a pastoral realm of primordial integrity. In the same way, the seventeenth century had shown its disapproval of the extremes of print culture in playing up the idea of the "inner light." Professor Abrams draws our attention to the "Cambridge Platonists" in this matter, striving to match the outer light from the book with the inner light of the spirit:

> Similar metaphors of mind were particularly prevalent in the philosophy of the "Cambridge Platonists" (more Plotinists, actually, than Platonists), whom Wordsworth had read, and Coleridge had studied intensively. In these writers, the familiar figure of the spirit of man as a candle of the Lord easily lent itself to envisioning the act of perception as that little candle throwing its beam into the external world. I shall cite excerpts from one chapter of Nathanael Culverwel's *An*

Elegant and Learned Discourse of the Light of Nature, because it serves as a convenient inventory of analogies for the mind as receptor or projector—as a mirror or lamp. The *Discourse* was written before general knowledge of the full implication of Hobbes's major works had sharpened the point at issue, and Culverwel sets out to represent "unto you, as *indifferently* as I can, the *state* of this great *Controversie.*" In this dispute he takes Plato and Aristotle to have been the chief protagonists.

"*Now the Spirit of man is the Candle of the Lord,*" he says, for the Creator, himself the "fountain of Light," furnished and beautified this "*lower part of the World with Intellectual Lamps,* that should shine forth to the *praise* and *honour* of his Name. . . ."

"The end of Poetry," wrote Wordsworth, "is to produce excitement in co-existence with an over-balance of pleasure. The effect of Poetry is to rectify men's feelings." The poets became ever more inclined to make their art a counterenvironment to the specialized ugliness that was growing around them. Professor Abrams observes:

143

> We are on the way, by this time, to the stereotype of the *poète maudit*, endowed with an ambiguous gift of sensibility which makes him at the same time more blessed and more cursed than the other members of a society from which he is, by the destiny of inheritance, an outcast.

The tendency, that is, of the Romantic artist is to become a probe into his society. At least as much as the scientist, the artist began to use his senses and his art as a laboratory means of investigation. The antisocial aura of the scientist and the artist tended to fuse, as the century moved on, with the image of the criminologist. Poe's Dupin is an aesthete and an integral investigator, like Poe and the Symbolists in general. Professor Abrams points out the cliché probing of poets:

> Coleridge, with considerable justification, has been called the master of the fragment. . . . Yet in criticism, what he took from other writers he developed into a speculative instrument

which, for its power of insight and, above all, of application in the detailed analysis of literary works, had no peer among the German organic theorists.

It was Coleridge's draft for an encyclopedia that gave Newman his *Idea of a University*, as Dwight Culler explains in *The Imperial Intellect*.

The history of science provides excellent material for observing the environmental groping of the scientist before the new paradigm, or hypothesis, can be pushed up into focal intensity:

> The history of electrical research in the first half of the eighteenth century provides a more concrete and better known example of the way a science develops before it acquires its first universally received paradigm. During that period there were almost as many views about the nature of electricity as there were important electrical experimenters, men like Hauksbee, Gray, Desaguliers, Du Fay, Nollett, Watson, Franklin, and others. All their numerous concepts of electricity had something in common—they were partially derived from one or another version of the mechanico-corpuscular philosophy that guided all scientific research of the day. In addition, all were components of real scientific theories, of theories that had been drawn in part from experiment and observation and that partially determined the choice and interpretation of additional problems undertaken in research. Yet though all the experiments were electrical and though most of the experimenters read each other's works, their theories had no more than a family resemblance.
>
> —Thomas S. Kuhn, *The Structure of Scientific Revolutions*

The main Cinderella plot of *My Fair Lady* (Lerner and Lowe's adaptation of Shaw's *Pygmalion*) is a retrieval of the nineteenth-century world of mechanical industry that had mass-produced a large new upper middle class. The industrial technique of precise repetition gets new force from the musical rhythms, which also increase the irony of dehumanization by which both mechanized speech and mechanized production are attained. This class had been provided with a special uniform speech by the new public

144

schools. It was a speech that unconsciously *mimed* the machine itself (as T. S. Eliot wittily observed when his Madame Sosostris speaks to her client: "Tell dear Mrs. Equitone . . ."). To speak with the mechanical precision of a machine has been an aspect of the comic mask worn by the corporate English upper class for some decades. To acquire this manner is not only easy but devastating. One puts on vocally the technology of the age, much as Chaplin did in his way, as if in revenge and reversal.

First American jazz and now the English Beatles have mechanically extended the speech modes of the lower middle classes with image-acceptance. For such mimetic enlargements of ordinary experience are as enticing and flattering clichés as the movie or the motor car.

The mime of mechanization is then the subplot in *My Fair Lady*. It is not archetypal so much as it is technological cliché. Being thus submerged, it gains intensity. If we can succeed here in understanding the strange process by which an ancient archetype can be transformed into an environmental cliché, we shall perhaps have obtained a basic insight into many other processes.

145

The Graduate was a smash success because the dramatic action mimes the new electric and tribalizing technology. Ben spurns "plastics." So with the Theater of the Absurd. Its discontinuities mime the new technology as much as the mosaic form of the telegraph press anticipated Symbolist and Surrealist processes.

MIMESIS, OR MAKING SENSE

The entire world of technology makes sense by miming the human body and faculties.

Most studies of mimesis, from Plato to Auerbach and Koestler, proceed on the assumption of matching inner and outer. Notable exceptions are found in E. H. Gombrich's *Art and Illusion* and Eric Havelock's *Preface to Plato*. The technique of continuous parallel that Eliot indicates as the essential myth-making form of mimesis in his classic essay "*Ulysses*, Order and Myth" simply tosses aside the idea of matching in favor of interface and metamorphosis. Plato had objected to the traditional, magical idea of mimesis. E. H. Gombrich illustrates how the new Euclidean demand for matching and representational illusion began to flourish in Plato's day. Havelock explains the pre-Platonic function of mimesis:

> Plato is describing a total technology of the preserved word . . . a state of total personal involvement and therefore of emotional identification with the substance of the poetised statement. . . . A modern student thinks he does well if he diverts a tiny fraction of his psychic powers to memorize a single sonnet of Shakespeare. He is not more lazy than his Greek counterpart. He simply pours his energy into book reading and learning through the use of his eyes instead of his ears. His Greek counterpart had to mobilize the psychic resources necessary to memorize Homer and the poets. . . . You threw yourself into the situation of Achilles, you identified with his grief or his anger. You yourself became Achilles and so did the reciter to whom you listened. Thirty years

later you could automatically quote what Achilles had said or what the poet had said about him. Such enormous powers of poetic memorization could be purchased only at the cost of total loss of objectivity. . . . This then is the master clue to Plato's choice of the word *mimesis* to describe the poetic experience. It focuses initially not on the artist's creative act but on his power to make his audience identify almost pathologically and certainly sympathetically with the content of what he is saying . . . what [Plato] is saying is that any poetised statement must be designed and recited in such a way as to make it a kind of drama within the soul both of the reciter and hence also of the audience. This kind of drama, this way of reliving experience in memory instead of analysing and understanding it, is for him the "enemy."

One of the etymologies of "matching" is "making" (mac-ian). This polarity is inherent in consciousness as such. Certainly in the cliché-to-archetype process, if cognition is matching our sensory experience with the outer world, re-cognition is a repeat of that process. We have seen how dreaming involves a *ricorso* of this waking experience of the day: "The unpurged images of day recede" (Yeats). The whole of *Finnegans Wake* is a *ricorso*, a scrubbing purgation or private and corporate experience in the collective "dreaming back." "Making sense" is a phrase that indicates repetition of some experience which yields a sudden truth or meaning. In *Le Démon de l'Anglogie* Mallarmé reveals a creative process as a recap of the actual stages of apprehension. That is, creativity is the parallel of cognition, a retracking of the labyrinth of sensation. Ancient mythology is packed with examples of this awareness. Daedalus, the mightiest maker or engineer of antiquity, contrived the labyrinth that enclosed the Minotaur. The first page of *A Portrait of the Artist as a Young Man* concerns the cognitive labyrinth as it is traversed by Stephen, the artist hero, in his first encounter with the Minotaur and the other scandals (cf. Greek etymology).

Stephen's surname is not Daedalus but "Dedalus," i.e., "dead all us." Joyce's last story in *Dubliners*, "The Dead," and the last lines of the *Portrait* explain the relation of the young artist to the

148

dead: "I go to encounter for the millionth time the reality of experience and to forge in the smithy of my soul the uncreated conscience of my race." This verbal implication of *ricorso*, the millions of repetitions of the cognitive labyrinth, which is traced on the first page of the *Portrait*, is the task of making sense, of waking the somnambulists in the labyrinth of cognition.

In recounting the making of "The Lake Isle of Innisfree," Yeats tells how he was contemplating an advertisement for soft drinks in a London shop window where a tiny ball was dancing on top of a jet of water to convey the sportive, emancipated quality of the beverage. While Yeats stood on the pavement in the eye-, ear-, and air-polluted metropolis, he proceeded to create an anti-environment, namely "innisfree," in order to make sense of the anarchy of the world about him. In the moment of creating the artistic probe of Innisfree, Yeats tossed London on the middenheap. Art is a cliché probe that scraps older environments in order to retrieve other clichés that have been tossed aside earlier.

Aristotelian mimesis confirms the James Joyce approach, since it is a kind of recap of natural processes, whether of making sense via cognition or of making a house by following the lines of Nature. For example, in the *Physics*, Book II, Chapter VIII, Aristotle writes: "Thus, if a house had been a thing made by Nature it would have been made in the same way as it is now by art; and if things made by Nature were made also by art, they would come to be in the same way as by Nature." Aristotle thus confirms the sacral quality of the cliché or artifact by aligning it with the cosmic forces, just as biologists say ontogeny recaps phylogeny, i.e., knowing and growing are one, which is of course the theme of *The Portrait* by Joyce.

Shakespeare repeats Aristotle in *The Winter's Tale* when he puts into the mouth of Perdita:

> For I have heard it said
> There is an art which in their piedness shares
> With great creating Nature.

To which Polixenes comments:

149

> Say there be;
> Yet Nature is made better by no mean
> But Nature makes that mean; so, over that art,
> Which you say adds to Nature, is an art
> That Nature makes.
>
> —*The Winter's Tale*, Act IV, Scene 3

The *Metaphysics* of Aristotle begins with the statement: "All men by Nature desire to know." An indication of this is in the delight we take in our senses; for even apart from their usefulness they are lived for themselves; biogeneticists say today that a growing organism, at every point in its growth, has to know what the whole organism is doing in order to develop. The consequences of the images are the images of the consequences. This involvement and polarity, knowing and growing, is both creative and destructive. Yeats extended this relation between art and Nature in his later works, as in "Sailing to Byzantium":

> Once out of Nature I shall never take
> My bodily form from any natural thing,
> But such a form as Grecian goldsmiths make
> Of hammered gold and gold enamelling
> To keep a drowsy Emperor awake . . .

Here, once again, is the theme of art as a means of the keenest awareness, capable of giving consciousness even to a bureaucrat. Aristotle on *The Soul* (Book III, Chapter VII) points to the analogy between art and knowledge: "It is not a stone which is present in the soul, but its form. It follows that the soul is analogous to the hand; for as the hand is a tool of tools, so the mind is a form of forms and sense, the form of sensible things."

By way of resonance and repetition, "The soul is in a way all existing things." As the hand, with its extensions, probes and shapes the physical environment, so the soul or mind, with its extensions of speech, probes and orders and retrieves the man-made environment of artifacts and archetypes.

A cliché is an act of consciousness: total consciousness is the sum of all the clichés of all the media or technologies we probe with.

THE
ONE
AND
THE
MINI

In contrast to private awareness, social consciousness is a process of scrapping, retrieving, and probing. The emphasis for the most part is upon retrieval and the accumulation of vast residues. With the development in the nineteenth century of many new technologies (clichés), the supremacy of unified print consciousness gave way to multiconsciousness. There was no garbage heap, no middenheap, there was no unconscious large enough to contain all of the materials generated by the breakdown of so much probing and environing. Numerous works of literature and art testify to the impact of the new multiconsciousness. Jarry's *Ubu Roi*, Eliot's *The Waste Land*, the opening chapters of Wyndham Lewis's *The Apes of God*, Joyce's *Finnegans Wake*, the entire literature of the Theater of the Absurd all give evidence of this overwhelming impact.

Douglas M. Davis points out the mini-art sensibility that drives everywhere in the 1960s and after, in paintings and sculpture, in music, in architecture, in city planning, in the university, in dress and fashion. Philosophy and management alike have yet to come to terms with the mini-module or the new structure of the electric age. Nevertheless, even in the abstruse arguments of the phenomenologists (funambulists), the Existentialists, and the logical positivists, they reveal no awareness of the problems imposed upon philosophy by multiconsciousness. However, in their attempts to deal with contemporary problems they arrive at a complexity which is philosophical breakdown. These people show themselves to be literally "simple-minded."

Newspapers handle these problems ironically and laconically:

MAN'S WOES BLAMED ON HIS THREE BRAINS
By Marilyn Dunlop, Star Staff Writer

KINGSTON—Man has three brains—not one—and he must co-ordinate them if he is to survive, Dr. Paul MacLean of the

National Institute of Mental Health, Bethesda, Md., said yesterday.

In a lecture here to the Ontario Mental Health Foundation, MacLean said man's "new mammalian brain" has only recently developed.

It speaks, writes, reads, solves social problems and can learn from what man sees—even dream, MacLean said.

But man also has two other brains. One is his ancient "reptilian brain" that works by ancestral memories and instinct. The other is the "old mammalian brain" that is concerned with food and sex as a means of preserving the species through multiplication.

He said the struggle for territory and self-preservation is obsolete under modern conditions—even dangerous—but the new mammalian brain has trouble getting passage across to the older brains.

—*Toronto Daily Star*, February 13, 1969

153

An attempt to deal with multiconsciousness among scientists is discussed by Thomas Kuhn in *The Structure of Scientific Revolutions* in the chapter "The Priority of Paradigms":

. . . Scentists work from models acquired through education and through subsequent exposure to the literature often without quite knowing or needing to know what characteristics have given these models the status of community paradigms. And because they do so, they need no full set of rules. The coherence displayed by the research tradition in which they participate may not imply even the existence of an underlying body of rules and assumptions that additional historical or philosophical investigation might uncover. That scientists do not usually ask or debate what makes a particular problem or solution legitimate tempts us to suppose that, at least intuitively, they know the answer. But it may only indicate that neither the question nor the answer is felt to be relevant to their research. Paradigms may be prior to, more binding, and more complete than any set of rules for research that could be unequivocally abstracted from them.

So far this point has been entirely theoretical: paradigms

could determine normal science without the intervention of discoverable rules. Let me now try to increase both its clarity and urgency by indicating some of the reasons for believing that paradigms actually do operate in this manner. The first, which has already been discussed quite fully, is the severe difficulty of discovering the rules that have guided particular normal-scientific traditions. That difficulty is very nearly the same as the one the philosopher encounters when he tries to say what all games have in common. The second, to which the first is really a corollary, is rooted in the nature of scientific education. Scientists, it should already be clear, never learn concepts, laws, and theories in the abstract and by themselves. Instead, these intellectual tools are from the start encountered in a historically and pedagogically prior unit that displays them with and through their applications. A new theory is always announced together with applications to some concrete range of natural phenomena; without them it would not be even a candidate for acceptance. . . .

The perceptions of scientists are as culturally conditioned as those of a school child or a sage. It is characteristic of recent generations to think of the scientist as free from cultural propaganda, so that it is a novelty to expose the assumptions hidden from scientists. For example, the effects of Western literacy in according the illusion of space as a uniform continuum collapsed very suddenly with the advent of non-Euclidean geometry and relativity theory. The switch from the visual space of the Euclidean culture into the resonant space of quantum mechanics is completely misunderstood by the physicists who use the new paradigm of resonance. They are not aware that acoustic space has unique physical properties (a perfect sphere whose center is everywhere and whose margins are nowhere). The result is that quantum physicists continue to make efforts at visualizing the nonvisual, constructing little iconic models of DNA particles and the like. It is not surprising that science has not a clue as to the nature of gravity and continues to ignore the simple fact that Newton discovered levity, not gravity—i.e. moon-pull, not earth-pull.

With the dynamics of the new high-speed reading techniques

(with speeds of from 1000 to 50,000 words per minute), the mini-art of the Gutenberg movable types becomes a form of multi-consciousness. The reader can program for himself any single prose level, or can orchestrate a group of levels, as his sensibilities suggest.

Douglas M. Davis in "The Dimensions of the Miniarts" discusses current developments in painting and sculpture and music as part of the total change in sensibility. As he describes them, the new arts of multiconscious man encompass every area of action in our culture. The Japanese paradigm of the module began long ago with the mats on the floor.

> There seems to be a reductive sensibility at work in our time, manifesting itself not only in painting and sculpture, but in avant-garde film, dance, theater, poetry, music, architecture, even in certain areas of our daily and political lives. At the core of this sensibility is an implacable, common-sense determination to find and exploit what is beyond reduction; to exchange manners, "style," tradition, even craftsmanship for the essential, for what the kids call the nittygritty. To a painter like Frank Stella, a sculptor like Donald Judd, this means trading illusion for physical presence; for a film-maker like Andy Warhol, a choreographer like Ann Halprin, a poet like Emmett Williams, a composer like La Monte Young, the exchange is similar in idea if not in medium.

155

The familiar ad form of rippling repetition of profiles, is an accessible example of the mini-module that is found in every electric structure, from space capsule to the modes of consciousness.

Mallarmé and Joyce are masters of this kind of verbal module which is achieved by pushing beyond semantic frontiers:

> "The clichés give way to words which have the value of rarity. The volutes of the sentences are transformed into atomized phrases so that each word, which is made as syntactically independent as possible, gleams with its own light . . . The number of themes becomes more and more restrictive, the world of concrete things becomes more and more fragile and tenuous, and, in an inversely proportionate manner, the content be-

comes more and more abnormal. Where originally there were narrative poems, descriptive or passionate, which directed the attention to a limited content, now there are poems which direct the attention to themselves, to the existence of the language in itself."

—Elémire Zolla, *The Eclipse of the Intellectual*

PARADOX

Ay, truly; for the power of beauty will sooner transform honesty from what it is to a bawd than the force of honesty can transform beauty into his likeness; this was sometime a paradox, but now the time gives it truth.

—*Hamlet*, Act III, Scene 1

Hamlet's quip now applies to the entire world of cliché and archetype under computer conditions.

We will soon be sending our children to the Orient to Westernize them.

—"Book of Peter Pan"

A gentleman is one who is never rude unintentionally.

—Oscar Wilde

Law makes long spokes of the short stakes of men.
Your well fenced out real estate of mind
No high flat of the nomad citizen
Looks over, or train leaves behind.

—William Empson, "Legal Fiction"

The whole of the cliché-to-archetype process could be considered as classical paradox in reversing the popular notion of poet and artist, even as Yeats does in "The Circus Animals' Desertion." The present probe tests cliché as the current technology, and the archetypal world as the "rag-and-bone shop" of old perceptions and techniques. In the electric age there are far too many clichés available for retrieval. The paradoxical result is the end of garbage or of "rag-and-bone" shops. As we tend to extend consciousness itself by the new technology, we probe all, and scrap all, in a deluge of fragments of cultures for creativity.

A more familiar genre of paradoxical probing is G. K. Chesterton's "The Donkey":

THE DONKEY

When fishes flew and forests walked
  And figs grew upon thorn,
Some moment when the moon was blood
  Then surely I was born.

With monstrous head and sickening cry
  And ears like errant wings,
The devil's walking parody
  On all four-footed things.

The tattered outlaw of the earth,
  Of ancient crooked will;
Starve, scourge, deride me: I am dumb,
  I keep my secret still.

Fools! For I also had my hour;
  One far fierce hour and sweet:
There was a shout about my ears,
  And palms before my feet.

Chesterton's entire vision was paradoxical because it was based on perception as process. G. K. knew that analogy was community, and that is why he was able to write what Etienne Gilson considers one of the best books on Aquinas. Chesterton observed of Shaw that there was no paradox in him whatever—his wildest statements were perfectly continuous and logical. Chesterton's style of paradox is familiar in such phrases as "Women refused to be dictated to so they went out and became stenographers," and "Any stigma's good enough to beat a dogma." Apart from the fact that Christianity has been paradoxical from its inception, there is one explicit paradox in Acts 26: 24, wherein Paul made his defense before King Agrippa and Festus. "And as he thus made his defense, Festus said with a loud voice: 'Paul, . . . your great learning is turning you mad.' " Paul had begun his oration at the beginning of Chapter 26: "Agrippa said to Paul, 'You have permission to speak for yourself.' Then Paul stretched out his hand and made his defense."

It may have escaped the scriptural commentators that Paul's stretching out his hand was the formal act of the *doctus orator*, the man trained in the skills of encyclopedic wisdom and eloquence: rhetoric, the open hand; dialectic, the closed fist. In the defense that Paul presented, Festus recognized the virtuosity of the fully trained encyclopedist of eloquent wisdom. His remark, therefore, "Your great learning is turning you mad," is a technical observation. It is a paradox in that erudition was classically regarded as a main source of wisdom and sanity.

The basis of all paradox, Christian and secular, is to be found in the sixth book of the *Physics* of Aristotle, to which Aquinas refers in his *Summa Theologica* I-II q.113, a.7, *ad quintum*. The question for Aquinas is whether justification by faith occurs instantly or gradually. Aquinas says it occurs instantly because— here he appeals to Aristotle's *Physics*—"the whole preceding time during which anything moves towards its form, it is under the opposite form." This is a biological principle illustrated in the remark of the caterpillar as it cynically observed the antics of the butterfly: "You'll never catch me up in one of those danged things!" Since paradox required the encyclopedic wisdom of the traditional orator, it became the tradition at Cambridge University that the Senior Wrangler, or the top graduate of each year, would defend a paradox.

Paradoxia Epidemica by Rosalie L. Colie offers an encyclopedic approach to the genre of paradox. Miss Colie observes: "The rhetorical paradox was an ancient form designed as *epideixis*, to show off the skill of an orator and to arouse the admiration of an audience, both at the outlandishness of the subject and the technical brilliance of the rhetorician."

Arthur Koestler, in *The Act of Creation*, stresses the paradox of discovery in science and links it with the nature of wit and humor quite independently of the classical genre paradox:

> The creative act of the humorist consisted in bringing about a momentary fusion between two habitually incompatible

matrices. Scientific discovery, as we shall presently see, can be described in very similar terms—as the permanent fusion of matrices of thought previously believed to be incompatible. Until the seventeenth century the Copernican hypothesis of the earth's motion was considered as obviously incompatible with commonsense experience; it was accordingly treated as a huge joke by the majority of Galileo's contemporaries. One of them, a famous wit, wrote: "The disputes of Signor Galileo have dissolved into alchemical smoke. So here we are at last, safely back on a solid earth, and we do not have to fly with it as so many ants crawling around a balloon."

Paradox had a special appeal in the Gutenberg age of casuistry: "The rhetorical paradox as a literary form had duplicity built into it."

The entire aesthetic of Wyndham Lewis presents the case for paradox, as in "Vortex No. One—Art Vortex—Be Thyself":

> You must talk with two tongues, if you do not wish to cause confusion.
>
> You must also learn, like a Circassian horseman, to change tongues in mid-career without falling to Earth.
>
> You must give the impression of two persuaders, standing each on a different hip—left hip, right hip—with four eyes vacillating concentrically at different angles upon the object chosen for subjugation.
>
> There is nothing so impressive as the number TWO.
>
> You must be a duet in everything.
>
> For, the Individual, the single object, and the isolated, is, you will admit, an absurdity.
>
> Why try and give the impression of a consistent and indivisible personality?
>
> ---
>
> You can establish yourself either as a Machine of two similar fraternal surfaces overlapping.
>
> Or, more sentimentally, you may postulate the relation of object and its shadow for your two selves.
>
> There is Yourself: and there is the Exterior World, that fat mass you browse on.

You knead it into an amorphous imitation of yourself inside yourself.

Sometimes you speak through its huskier mouth, sometimes through yours.

Do not confuse yourself with it, or weaken the esoteric lines of fine original being.

Do not marry it, either, to a maiden.

Any machine then you like: but become mechanical by fundamental <u>dual</u> repetition.

For the sake of your good looks you must become a machine.

Hurry up and get into this harmonious and sane duality . . .

It is even more complicated than Mr. Eliot's tactic of standing on both sides of a mirror simultaneously. Miss Colie also notes: ". . . paradox equivocates. It lies, and it doesn't. It tells the truth, and it doesn't. . . . The one meaning must always be taken with respect to the other—so that the Liar paradox is, literally, speculative, its meanings infinitely mirrored, infinitely reflected, in each other."

In cliché-archetype terms, the paradox is a major form of cliché-probe dependent upon an encyclopedic retrieval of older clichés for its exercise. No more extreme instance of this process can be imagined than Joyce's discovery of the mirror as wheel:

I am glad you liked my punctuality as an engine driver. I have taken this up because I am really one of the greatest engineers, if not the greatest, in the world besides being a musicmaker, philosophist and heaps of other things. All the engines I know are wrong. Simplicity. I am making an engine with only one wheel. No spokes of course. The wheel is a perfect square. You see what I am driving at, don't you? I am awfully solemn about it, mind you, so you must not think it a silly story about the mouse and the grapes. No, it's a wheel, I tell the world. *And* it's all *square*.

In order to be as modern as possible at all times, Joyce turned to the ancient and classical modes of paradox, to learn both how to discover and how to instruct, enabling him to teach his readers the same arts:

> My remarks about the engine were not meant as a hint at the title. I meant that I wanted to take up several other arts and crafts and teach everybody how to do everything properly so as to be in the fashion.

Like Alice, Joyce pushed all the way through the Narcissus looking-glass. He moved from the private Stephen Dedalus to the Finnegan corporate image. The mirror, like the mind, by taking in and feeding back the same image becomes a wheel, a cycle, able to retrieve all experience.

In order to defend any paradox the wit needs to depend on memory, as Oscar Wilde pointed out. And so it is in science. Without a wide knowledge of the scrapped hypotheses of one's predecessors, discoveries would be difficult. Newton's idea of gravity was levity, i.e., not down, but upward and outward. For his discovery he was dubbed "a gothic ape" since he seemed to be a reactionary appealing to the "invisible" qualities of the school-men.

163

Another key facet of paradox is cited by Rosalie Colie as "what I call the epistemological paradox, in which the mind, by its own operation, attempts to say something about its operation."

Bacon's essay *Of Truth* illustrates his awareness of the epistemological paradox, for in developing an essay on this theme he treats the paradox as follows: "Though men consider truth as the *summum bonum*, they nevertheless have a very great fondness for the lie."

The whole of *Finnegans Wake*, including the title, is paradox; based on what Joyce considered man's greatest invention—the mirror of language, the "magazine wall" of memory and all human residue.

The cliché-probe aspect of paradox is stressed by Rosalie Colie: ". . . especially logical and mathematical paradoxes, are often 'fixed' into adamantine hardness, because they mark a regular edge to progressive thinking, a point at which 'object' turns into 'subject.' "

The "edge" of the "feed-forward" cliché-probe is always at the "interface" of discourse, but always engaged in retrieving old clichés from every sphere of human activity. As we have often said, there is a paradox in cliché itself, since at the moment of truth it is tossed onto the scrap heap of the obvious and the useless. In retrospect, all great discoveries are obvious.

In discussing the *Parmenides*, Rosalie Colie points out: "Paradoxes earn their right to question technique and method. . . . Once more, then, paradoxes turn out to be paradoxical, to do two things at once, two things which contradict or cancel one another." Thus, it is not only cliché that is paradoxical in its doubleness, but archetype as well. As Yeats insists, it is the "rag-and-bone shop" that is the source of the highest vision.

Utopias are paradoxes: "Literally, 'utopia' involves a negative statement . . . is the place which is not . . . What 'happens' in utopias is made up of elements opposite to the societies in which their authors had to live, looking-glass reflections on the defective real world."

164

It is, of course, no place (Eu-topia) is a good place. But today there have been many anti-Utopias written, just as our novels are full of anti-heroes. Rosalie Colie illustrates that Utopias can be put in very brief form, as in Marvell's "Upon Appleton House": ". . . the annual flooding the Nunappleton fields by the River Denton, creating a topsy-turvy world where

"Boats can over Bridges sail;
And Fishes do the Stables scale."

Miss Colie points out: "The meadows are both a disrupted world . . . and, in the reflecting surface of the flood, a looking-glass world. . . ."

Lewis Carroll's looking-glass world is much more sophisticated, since in going through the looking-glass one goes from a world of three dimensions to one of many dimensions of non-Euclidean space. Carroll was a mathematician familiar with the geometry of Lobachevski.

Miss Colie discusses More's *Utopia* as ". . . written first as a very short book, its contents only the present second part, the utopian section: later, to bring his model commonwealth into higher relief, More added in the first book the description of his actual England." Miss Colie is apparently unaware of the "little epic" form which More is employing. The epyllion, by creating an interface or continuous parallel between two worlds, one past, one present, is a mythic, motivational genre of the greatest importance in the history of European literatures. It never had a higher cultivation than in the twentieth century. More's Book I is the retrieval of the medieval archetype world, and his Book II is the cliché-probe of his own time, retrieving the past.

The Praise of Folly by Erasmus is, she observes, ". . . obviously a praise of something conventionally regarded as unworthy of a proper oration." Miss Colie seems to be unacquainted with the tradition of Fools in Christ, the *idiotes*, a tradition which reached one of its classical manifestations in Dostoevski's *The Idiot*. Once more the praise of current corruptions is a cliché-probe for retrieving the ancient follies of the schoolmen and beyond. As in the *Epistolae Obscurorum Vivorum*, there is a little-epic relation between two worlds, creating a comic myth.

165

Sir Thomas Browne, in his adherence to Tertullian's test of theological truth, *"Certum est, quia impossibile est,"* is really keeping open for himself the possibility of further exploration in any or all directions. In his *Religio Medici*, paradox is multiplied. It is not easy to discover just what species of writing Browne engaged in in this work. The title would indicate the religion of a doctor, but although Browne was a doctor, he didn't give this title to his essay. Whoever gave the title to this work when it was pirated perceived paradox in Browne's position as a medical student. Browne himself, at the beginning of the *Religio Medici*, calls attention to the scandal of his profession—the reputation that medical practitioners had for free-thinking. The work, when examined closely, is a set of variations upon a theme—that if a virtue is pushed far enough, it becomes a vice. He uses this cliché to retrieve many archetypes and much learning. Browne is with the scientists in their inquiry into the Book of Nature; but he is against them when they use modesty or a "circumspect method of inquiry" to denude or desecrate human nature. As an amphibian swimming in a world of religion and natural philosophy, Browne suffers the fate of being rejected by both religionists and by scientists. He was put on the index as a heretic, and he did not succeed in gaining entry into the Royal Society, an appointment which he coveted.

Bishop Sprat, in his defense of the Royal Society in 1667, is paradoxical in a more mediocre way, associating himself with the artisans and shopkeepers of England, in his belief that the new corporate science must draw upon this social class for its members. He reassures his readers that there is nothing irreligious in a materialistic inquiry into Nature's truths. "Natural philosophy," he declares, "is the highest priority, because it is an inquiry into God's will." This he reveals in his second book of *Revelation, the Book of Nature.*

Paradox was the means by which early theological science made its discoveries. Paradox is the posture of the mind when, like a boxer balanced on two feet, it is feinting for an opening. Scientific discovery is always attended by paradox. Newtonian science, with its "circumspect" experimental method, assumes that God is both rational and arbitrary.

Darwinian theory supposes that species can evolve but still persist in a world where all is change—it is a theory at once radically revolutionary and radically conservative. Equally para-doxical is Ludwig von Bertalanffy, whose contribution to general systems theory ranks with the epoch-making discoveries of scien-tists of the past: "In open systems, we have not only *entropy production* owing to irreversible processes taking place in the system: we have also *entropy transport*, by way of introduction of material which may carry high free energy or 'negative entropy.' "

PARODY

Imitation is the sincerest form of battery.

Aristotle is silent.

—H. H. Watts, *The Sense of Regain*

For many people, travesty is a synonym for parody. Travesty means literally a "transvestite" and has some relevance to parody since by changing one's garbage of environment one sets up a parallel with another environment. The interplay of environments is translation; the Latin word is *translatio,* and the Greek word is *metaphorein* (which appears on moving vans in Toronto as *metapheri*).

Movie critics have pointed out that Mae West (she was a visual pun!) impersonated a female impersonator. This may have obtained for her the unexpected honor of having an environmental garment named after her. The "Mae West" was no matter of mere levity, but a protection against graver depth charges.

Robert Coryat, the Elizabethan traveler, reported that he "found Venetian actresses almost as good as the Elizabethan boy actors."

I like it not when a woman hath a grey beard.

—*The Merry Wives of Windsor*

Parody can be an approach to anything from "fake Vermeers" to "fake Rembrandts" or "fake Van Goghs." These fakes don't endanger the world of perception or art, but they do endanger the market. Suppose a fake Shakespeare were to be "discovered"? A play quite up to the quality of his, say, middle period but unlike anything that we have of his? Would this be a *bad* thing?

A parody is new vision. When Dryden drew a parallel to the

Old Testament narrative of King David and Absalom in his *Absalom and Achitophel* he was creating a parallel between the contemporary and the past which lent a great force to the political critique of the present. "Parody" is one road running beside another road (*para hodos*). The new Gutenberg cliché retrieved medieval romances, creating a massive parallel between the medieval and Renaissance audiences for these works. Cervantes seized upon this new cliché to probe the present. All of Shakespeare's historical plays must be regarded as probes of the Elizabethan England contemporary to him. Queen Elizabeth remarked to an ambassador, "I am Richard II." Marlowe's *Edward II* draws attention to the impossible position of a female ruler in an authoritarian masculine age. This play was a critique of Elizabeth I via the metaphor of homosexuality.

Professor Barbara De Luna has devoted an entire study to Ben Jonson's Catiline as a "parallelograph" or parody of the Catiline conspiracy with reference to the gunpowder plot. So powerful was this Ben Jonson parody, Professor De Luna declares, that it became the most talked-about play of the first half of the 1600s.

169

The "scale model" in our contemporary design sense may have been used by Virgil in his "Gnat" or as it is used in the first two books of *Gulliver's Travels*.

Max Black in *Models and Metaphors* provides a useful approach to the subject when he distinguishes between the scientist's use of scale models and analogue models. He points out that the scale model is essentially simile, but that the analogue model is true metaphor.

Some parody has the tepidity of simile; some parody has the force of metaphor. *Gulliver's Travels* seems to be a scale model but actually is highly metaphoric. *True Grit* is a parody of the Western in which scenery is given travelogue beauty intensity, acting as the subplot for a slob world of goalless individualists.

Lewis Carroll presents his fake world as a realistic scale model. "Realism" implies dominance of visual and other sensory detail. *Sweeney Agonistes* is a parody of a parody based, on one hand, on Aristophanic comic mode and, on the other, on Victorian melodrama. The whole classical parallel is in turn made parallel to the Frenzy of Suibhne. Michael O'Brien noted that Sweeney, the Boston Irishman as caricature caveman, afforded just such a parallel between contemporaneity and antiquity as Eliot welcomed in Joyce's *Ulysses*. *The Frency of Suibhne* was published in a translation from the Gaelic by the Irish Text Society in 1913: "Many of the themes of the poem in which Sweeney appears are included in capsule form in the two epigraphs to *Sweeney Agonistes*."

Shakespeare's sonnets parody the Petrarchan Love Game and, as they do so, probe Shakespeare's major interest in the Machiavellian desacralization of Elizabethan life. Shakespeare's Falstaff is the parodic thief of the macro-thief or usurper whose name is Henry IV, the deposer of Richard II. The popular phrase "It takes a thief to catch a thief" indicates a parallel that inheres in our whole cult of the anti-hero. This abbreviated form of parody pervades Joyce: "Casting her perils before swains," or "Spitz on the iern while it's hot."

170

Professor E. S. Carpenter, the anthropologist, tells of native wood craftsmen who contrived most elaborate structures. When asked to box them for shipment, they were at a loss. The idea of putting the complex spaces of their carvings inside a plain cubic container was an entire novelty to them. Putting one space inside another space seemed to them as if making a parody of their own work. The idea of enclosed space is alien to the complex sensuous spaces of nonliterate men. Sigfried Giedion explains in *The Beginnings of Architecture* that the Romans were the first and only people ever to enclose space in the ancient world—by putting the arch inside a rectangle.

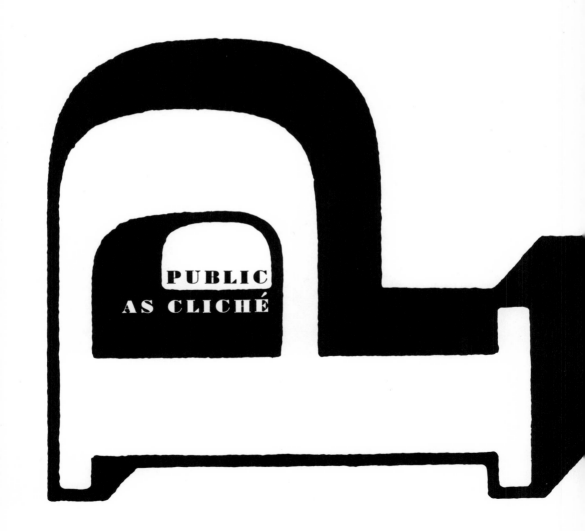

PUBLIC
AS CLICHÉ

"This must be fate! I've always considered myself
the average reader, and you the average author."

I was very much impressed to discover how the public in a big city is actually formed. It lives in a tumult of money making and dispersive activities and what we call emotion can neither be expressed nor communicated. All the pleasures, even the theatre, must simply distract . . . I seem to have noted an aversion to poetic productions, at least to the degree in which they are poetic, which seems to me quite natural precisely for these reasons. Poetry demands meditation, isolates man against his will, it crops up again and again, and in the vast world (not to say the large one) it is as uncomfortable as a faithful mistress.

—Goethe to Schiller, August 9, 1797

Discussing the question of how the readers of fiction may use it to gain access to a finer code than their own, Q. D. Leavis cites a letter that puts cliché and archetype in a new relation of complementarity, explaining:

> . . . what the cheaper forms of literature really do achieve for those to whom they appeal. (Speaking as one of the herd to whom Priestley and Walpole have meant a good deal, these last five years, and Eliot and Lawrence practically nil, and who can quite honestly read P. G. Wodehouse with profit) I am not sure that you do not underestimate the extent to which the existence of any real channel of "communication" between any artist and his public depends on his managing a symbolisation of something which was previously the property of that public: in this sense the crime of "giving the public what it wants" has another and not necessarily evil meaning (though this does not justify the usual or Northcliffe idea of doing so). I think the intrinsic qualities of a work of art are impotent unless they can symbolise, reflect, and focus in a convenient form, something that is already to some extent present in the mind of the man who hears, sees, or reads the work. Thus any art that I appreciate appeals because it

symbolises (not necessarily formulates explicitly) something that is already in my fund of experience. That is why a writer like Walpole, who is probably not sensitive to more than the common doings of rather common people, is to me a very great man, whose greatness is never really likely to be approached by artists whose work can only symbolise, or evoke the response of, a sensitivity that I and the vast majority have never experienced. I have been enormously impressed by Priestley's latest book because, I think, it succeeds in symbolising, and thus coheres and concentrates, some knowledge I already had in a dim and confused way, *e.g.* that most people, as uneducated as myself, are a curious mixture of the comic, the pathetic, and the tragic, are moved chiefly by little things of which they ought to take no notice, are preoccupied constantly and frequently inspired or terrified, by the unnecessary, the trivial and the accidental, and have no conscious sense of values about anything, and most of all dislike trying to think about anything subtle.

174

Throughout the entire discussion of *Fiction and the Reading Public* Mrs. Leavis makes the assumption of a "higher code" which it is the function of literature to make accessible. Entrée via this code is presumed sufficient to enable the reader to "place" the products and activities of any culture at all. Mrs. Leavis is making the familiar literary assumption that matching, rather than making, is the function of literary training. In a world of rapid innovation and environmental development the "finer code" permits the classification of novelties and the rejection of vulgarity, but for the creation of new codes from new cultural materials, the finer code, as a mere matching or checking device, is quite ineffectual. Indeed, the "finer code" that Mrs. Leavis finds so adequately manifested in the homogeneous tonalities of eighteenth-century prose is an interesting example of the environmental form being moved up to nostalgic archetypal status by a nineteenth-century mind. It is the nineteenth century that discovers rich cultural values in the ritual gestures and corporate decorum of eighteenth-century discourse. The twentieth century, on the other hand, has discovered many new values in the popular art and literature of the nineteenth century.

Hopkins, for example, abandoned the corporate uses of language as social mask, or manner, using words and phrases as heuristic probes with which to explore and to restore the hidden sinews of English.

What appears to elude the Leavis approach is the role of ever-new art and literature in creating new perception for new environments. Such environments are invisible and invincible except as they are raised to consciousness by new artistic styles and probes. With the advent of new styles or instruments of perception, the effect of the new environment is to mirror the image of the old one. The industrial nineteenth century developed a considerable empathy for anthropology and the study of nonliterate societies. Industrial and print technology have a profoundly fragmenting effect on human sensibilities. It was not, therefore, very realistic to use non-literate societies as a "mirror of Perseus" in which to observe the hated face of the industrial Gorgon. The great merit of *Fiction and the Reading Public* is in its concentration upon the changing audiences for fiction. It is a piece of audience research that has done much to get attention for literature as a changing social mask. Literature as a consumer commodity is an inevitable development of an age of industrial mass production. Such a world is ingenious in devising ever-new packages:

175

> In effect, every magazine is a package, labelled and au-
> thoritatively sealed with the symbol of the editor's approval.
> . . . The young author is often confused by a rejection which
> simply says, "This is not a *Harper* story." That does not
> mean it is not a good story; it simply means that the tale
> does not, in the editor's trained mind, conform to the type of
> fiction which his magazine has established.

Exploration of the function of audience forms is not easy for literary people who can understand only "content." The poet, or creator, more than the critic, tries to exploit new technology in order to establish new plateaus for perception. The critic tends rather to look at the values of the preceding age which have been eroded by the new developments. The critic is like the accountant adding up profits and losses. He is tempted to admonish the young to hold their fingers firmly in the eighteenth-century dike of a society with critical standards firmly imposed by the mandarinate. It was essentially an aristocratic culture, so that the mere idea of any serious challenge to it was almost unthinkable. The eighteenth century had, in its turn, derived the habit of seriousness from the seventeenth:

> The Puritan conscience implied a seriousness, an habitual occupation of the mind by major questions, and this had been the shaping factor in the lives of the middle-class and respectable poor from Bunyan's age till well on into the nineteenth century, when, as we have seen, it was side-tracked into a path which has more and more widely diverged from that of the arts. . . .

It should be clear, however, that standards imposed from above can have little value in relating people to one another in environments that have never existed before. The creative value of commercial stereotypes appears in the portrait of Gerty MacDowell in Joyce's *Ulysses*. Gerty is a mosaic of banalities that reveals the effect of these forms in shaping and extending our lives. Joyce enables the reader to exult and triumph over the trivia by letting him in on the very process by which they dramatize our lives. In the same way, in the newspaper, or "Aeolus," episode of *Ulysses*, Joyce deploys for us the world of verbal gimmicks as well as the mechanical operations upon which they depend. He floods the entire newsmaking situation with an intelligibility that provides a catharsis for the accumulated effects of the stereotypes in our lives.

There are various nostalgic perspectives in *Fiction and the Reading Public* that are relevant to an understanding of the processes of cliché and archetype:

> . . . it would not be true to suggest a stratification of novel writers and novel readers in 1760, for example, when any one who could read would be equally likely to read any novel, or every novel, published, and the only division of the novelists of that age that can be made is between good and indifferent (effective and ineffective); even a century later the same conditions hold, for though at that time Dickens,

Reade, and Wilkie Collins were the idols of the man in the
street and George Eliot and Trollope of the educated, yet each
class read or perfectly well might have read the entire output
of all the contemporary novelists, who all live in the same
world, as it were, understand each other's language, live by
the same code, and employ a common technique presenting no
peculiar difficulty to the reader.

Is it not strange that Mrs. Leavis should find values in the past
cultural uniformity of a mechanical society just when much greater
integration of the public had occurred via telegraph? The quality
of past industrial homogeneity has now acquired archetypal status,
thanks to the powerful electric environment of retribalized man.
This new electric service environment of oral culture enables us
to perceive value in archaic communities where everybody shares
a large body of traditional lore and experience. Plainly, however,
an integral society, whether tribal or civilized, oral or literate, is
possibly only under conditions of much continuity of external
organization.

177

The function of art in a tribal society is not to orient the population to novelty but to merge it with the cosmos. Value does not
inhere in art as object but in its power to educate the perceptions.
In a homogeneous mechanized society, the individualist role of
the training of perception scarcely exists. The primitive role of art
of serving as consolidator and as liaison with the hidden cosmic
powers again comes to the fore in popular art. Paradoxically, it is
the most vulgar art that has the most in common with the integral
societies of preliterate man. It is unfortunate, therefore, to invoke
homogeneity as a distinct excellence of so civilized a society as
that of the eighteenth century.

This merely tends to draw attention to the process of typographic
fragmentation by which the eighteenth century achieved its homogeneity. Such was the process by which uniform prices and extensive markets were created. The same marked processes were
extended to literature. They had begun in the first place in print
technology, without which neither industry nor markets could
exist. It is not very satisfactory to concur in one part of this process
and to reject the rest.

Regarding Tragedy and Comedy, any factor that alienates an individual from his environment archetypalizes him as tragic. Job loses his possessions and his family. Any individual bereaved by a traffic accident is similarly alienated from his environment: viz., *The Stranger* by Camus, *The Outsider* by Colin Wilson, Oedipus, etc. Comedy, on the other hand, seems to imply the reverse movement of the individual toward the group. The individual becomes environmental. Like W. B. Yeats in Auden's poem, "He became his admirers."

The complaint about Virginia Woolf—"Why, you can't read her unless your mind is absolutely fresh!"—draws attention to the print medium in a very special way. The mere act of reading is itself a lulling and semi-hypnotic experience. The further fact that print has long been a major environmental factor renders it invisible save to the artist. When the Symbolists began to deal with words as things, they bypassed the print process and accepted words as pigment, as textures, as structures with auras of many kinds. All of these strategies were necessary in order to encounter words at all in the typographic environment.

Mrs. Leavis' complaint about the world of Ethel M. Dell (or Tarzan) as programing for the print medium is irrelevant since these kinds of "content" are in fact perfectly adjusted to the quality of print itself, as it affects the sensibilities of our time. Why has it never occurred to the literary public that a monotonous and hypnotic use of print might be the main cause attracting content to suit? It was already clear to Alexander Pope at the beginning of the eighteenth century that, as print became more environmental, an inky fog had settled down over the human consciousness.

Is it not natural that, as any form whatever becomes environmental and unconscious, it should select as "content" the most common and vulgar and environmental of materials? As any form becomes environmental, it tends to be soporific. That is why its content must also become innocuous in order to match the effects of the medium. Any medium whatever, as it becomes pervasive, is to that degree common and vulgar and therefore attracts and demands only common and vulgar materials. To the artist this vulgarity is an opportunity so far as he is competent to set it in opposition to another equally pervasive form. Since the artist is typically interested in revealing forms, he never balks at contact with the most vulgar materials. The play within the play in *Hamlet* is a tissue of sixteenth-century banalities and clichés, as indeed was most of *Hamlet* to the Elizabethan. The encounter of one kind of environmental cliché with another leads to revolution as an art form. Michael Harrington sees the consequences:

> This accidental revolution is the sweeping and unprecedented technological transformation of the Western environment which has been, and is being carried out in a casual way. . . . Conservatives made a revolution, but it was not the one the revolutionists had predicted, and the antagonists were mutually bewildered. . . . Literacy increased, making many educators fearful, since its uses seemed anticultural; the people asserted themselves and the traditional democrats became uneasy. There was perplexity on all sides.

179

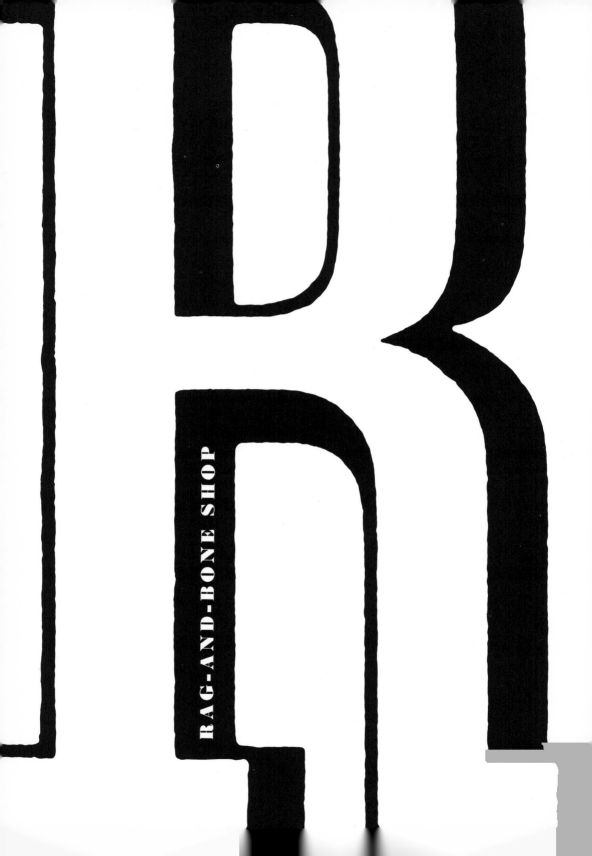

RAG-AND-BONE SHOP

Those masterful images because complete
Grew in pure mind, but out of what began?
A mound of refuse or the sweeping of a street,
Old kettles, old bottles, and a broken can,
Old iron, old bones, old rags, that raving slut
Who keeps the till. Now that my ladder's gone,
I must lie down where all the ladders start,
In the foul rag-and-bone shop of the heart.

—W. B. Yeats, "The Circus Animals' Desertion"

181

Help beautify Junk Yards
Throw Something Lovely Away Today.

—Sign outside a Toronto junkyard

Emma Lazarus's famous poem which is engraved on the Statue of
Liberty concludes:

   . . . Give me your tired, your poor,
   Your huddled masses yearning to breathe free,
   The wretched refuse of your teeming shore.
   Send these, the homeless, tempest-tossed to me:
   I lift my lamp beside the golden door.

A headline in the *Toronto Telegram* of March 5, 1969:

METRO GARBAGE MAY ONE DAY
BE USED AS BUILDING BLOCKS

The same principle applied at the educational level is indicated in the *Toronto Daily Star* of March 15, 1969:

PHILADELPHIA SCHOOL USES
WHOLE CITY AS ITS CLASSROOMS

Stratton Holland, describing one of the most significant experiments in North America, observes shrewly (lewd and loud), "The big saving is in the school building."

The Scandinavians long ago discovered that the ideal playfield for children was a high heap of old cars and discarded equipment. The city as a total environment is the ungraded and unstructured school *in excelsis*. No wonder the Watts kids said, "Why should we go to school and interrupt our education?"

Today, in the much greater junkyard of entertainment and advertising presented on radio and television, the child has access to every corner of the cultures of the world, past and present. Roaming this vast jungle as a "hunter," the child feels like a primitive native of a totally new kind of environment. When he encounters older educational hardware (schools and structured courses), he responds exactly as natives have always done to colonial and imperial exploiters of their unstructured "thing." He says, with an eye cocked at the satellite proscenium arch, "The globe is my theater. I shall not want for parts nor pastures."

Recent archaeological discoveries show that the Trojans who inhabited some of the Troys which were built on the site of Homeric Troy were accustomed to throwing away their garbage, mostly bones, in their houses. When the debris became objectionably high, they simply trampled it down and raised the roof of the dwelling place. There is some suggestion that the Troy of Homer's *Iliad* dealt with its garbage in this barbaric way.

Joyce's *Wake* works on the pattern of "one world burrowing on another": "Toborrow and toburrow and tobarrow! That's our crass, hairy and ever-grim life, till one finel howdiedow Bouncer Naster raps on the bell with a bone and his stinkers stank behind him with the sceptre and the hourglass."

The classification of "garbage" concerns a host of misconceptions. The term itself literally signifies clothing. The cultures of the world have been clad in and constituted by retrieved castoffs: "These fragments I have shored against my ruins." All the epic poems of the world are ingeniously assembled fragments of script cultures.

The *Random House Dictionary of the English Language* (1966) assigns the fifth meaning of "garbage" to that new global environment of cast-off nose cones, boosters, and other ballistic flotsam and jetsam.

New York magazine for March 10, 1969, is devoted to "The Trash Explosion." "One man's trash is another man's treasure," as indicated by a shop in Greenwich Village named "Bridgewater! Trash and Treasures." The feature piece is by Paul Wilkes: "The Garbage Apocalypse." "The day is fast approaching when there will be no more land we can reclaim with our refuse. . . . The official word is that we have up to eight years. The unofficial word is four years."

183

Mr. Wilkes adds: "Can industries will continue to appoint committees to advance the problem, while they grind out billions of one-way containers." It's as if the environment had become the Container Corpse of America (the container revolution—a new cliché world for retrieving of gourmet goodies of many cultures). The container cliché scrapped the grocer with his measuring scoop and scales and wrapping paper. By pushing the "package" cliché to a point of no return, we have made the entire world ours for the packaging. The container "corpse" can be put on ice and postponed for future generations.

In 1969, Container Corporation was included in the Montgomery Ward package. It scrapped and rewrapped itself.

The Gutenberg innovation scrapped the medieval world and dumped classical antiquity in the Renaissance lap. Today electric retrieval systems scrap nineteenth-century mechanism and dump the entire collection of archaic and preliterate cultures on the

Western doorstep. Electronic culture has created the multiprobe, and this probe results in vast amounts of garbage. The new information environment scraps the university, returning it, as it were, to its primal state. The large business corporations dissolve into connubiums and consortiums; just as large empires become congeries of mini-states. The ABM systems are designed to junk the ICBM systems of other powers. This pattern, in which a cliché-probe junks present environments, is to be seen in other areas of modern culture. In literature, works like Eliot's *The Waste Land*, Joyce's *Finnegans Wake*, and Beckett's *Waiting for Godot* are concerned with the destructive aspects of the enormous creativity of the electronic age. All of Pop art, Funk art, Op art, and the various other versions of mini-art reiterate the process by which cliché-probe destroys and creates. At the conclusion of "The Circus Animals' Desertion" Yeats perhaps suggests the renewal which he doesn't actually specify:

> I must lie down where all the ladders start,
> In the foul rag-and-bone shop of the heart.

How to elicit creativity from these middenheaps has become the problem of modern culture.

Perhaps one of the ways to its solution is indicated in the area of clothing. The "flower people" have set a new fashion which may be a paradigm for the entire global culture. They have substituted costumes for dress, role-playing for job-holding. The mini-skirt is not a fashion, and "unisex" is not homosexual. Retribulation is the universal mode in every kind of organization, regardless of geography or ideology.

The cause is the speed-up of information movement to instant levels. The resulting "inflation" of cultural currency creates a corresponding decline in all residual or establishment areas. Summer school, for example, or a third semester, speeds student turnover and lowers the levels of dialogue for teacher and student alike. Bureaucracy increases quickly in such schools. The "flower people," likewise, will soon take over the bureaucratic function of state and army in order to propagate peace and Peter Pan.

RETRIEVAL

History is bunk.

—Henry Ford

"Well, back to unravel mystery of honorable steam engine."

The changing of the day into night, the seasons, the flowers, the fruits, and all the rest which comes to us from time to time so that we can and must enjoy them—these are the true impulses toward life on earth. The more we are open to such pleasures the happier we are. If, however, this variety of sights dances before our eyes without our taking part in them, if we are not receptive to these sacred offerings, then the great evil finds its way into us, the most severe sickness: we consider life a repulsive burden.

—Goethe, *Poetry and Truth*

In *The Sacred and the Profane: The Nature of Religion* Mircea Eliade writes a sort of manifesto against the "secular city" that is significant for the cliché-to-archetype process. In the age of electric technology, the age of the zero gradient, the sacred or divine city of the ancient and native cultures is given archetypal status. In the environment created by electric circuitry, the entire world takes on again the dimensions of a "divine animal." All the fragmentation of the Neolithic technologies begins to appear as a profanation of this divine animal. This would seem to be a fairly clear-cut case of nostalgic archetypalizing, characteristic of all Utopias. Even Orwell's *1984* enshrines the nineteenth century, not the present or future.

187

David Bazelon's *The Paper Economy* is a fascinating example of a book that archetypalizes a preceding technology. In a world of electronic information, in which credit has already supplanted currency in a high degree, the old money and contractual arrangements have begun to assume the character of the Model T. They are ready for the museum.

> The seeds of every new society are to be discerned, after the fact, in the precedent order. There was a kernel of managerialism—servants-more-important-than-masters—in capitalist society from the beginning. The first managerialists, on

the thing side, were the independent intellectuals, the inventors and other creators of modern technology; and the lawyers, on the people side, accompanied and followed by the bankers and other financial people. When a new order forms itself within the old, the process will be obscured by the fact, among others, that certain people identified as Leading Citizens of the old order will fill roles defined by and devoted to the new order. (This may be done unconsciously: it is not less effective thereby.) Describing an earlier transition, Burnham emphasized that "in some, not a few, cases the capitalists came from the ranks of the old ruling class, from among the feudal lords themselves."

SPEAKING IN QUOTES

Organized charity in North America is like a boy who has grown too big for his boots.

—Toronto *Globe and Mail*

When anyone is "too big for his britches," it is understood that somewhat earlier he was *not* too big. These popular phrases indicate a special kind of insight into the cliché-archetype processes. The new situation has an effect on the older one such as to cause the enlarged person to take himself much more seriously. Susan Sontag, writing notes on "Camp" in her *Against Interpretation* observes:

> Camp sees everything in quotation marks. It's not a lamp, but a "lamp"; not a woman, but a "woman." To perceive Camp in objects and persons is to understand Being-as-Playing-a-Role. It is the farthest extension, in sensibility, of the metaphor of life as theater.

"Camp" is a kind of dropoutism resulting from the new electric environment. All the earlier forms go into quotes, as it were, when they have this new world to encompass them. Even camping out is a form of dropoutism made possible by varieties of new artificial environments created by new gadgets. The Eskimo found it possible to live in an igloo when he acquired the primus stove from the white invaders of his culture. The primus stove created, as it were, the igloo as a new decentralized and expendable house. This was pointed out to me long ago by Professor E. S. Carpenter, whose book *Eskimo* is a study of the special space and time senses of the Eskimo. Not only did the primus stove make possible the igloo as habitation, but the white man's demand for furs provided the incentive for the Eskimo to form trapping lines and to camp out. Normally, the Eskimo lives in a stone house. Trapping encouraged the igloo as camp, or a quickie home.

"Camp" is not a form of retrieval but rather simply rear-view-mirror nostalgia. It is not a new service environment or cliché, but a means of escaping into the gingerbread world of Mom and nursery.

Print as a means of retrieving the past was unrivaled in scope and intensity, and made available the entire world of antiquity, which had been only slightly accessible in manuscript form. It also made available the entire world of scholasticism, which, for the most part, had been an oral form of culture based on sententious aphorism. The new speed and repetition of the presses also poured forth the world of the illuminated manuscripts and the Books of Hours. The creation of the new reading public by the printing press meant also an entirely new world of genre in the arts. Cervantes and Rabelais explored these changes in the reading public as the effect of the mixture of genres on a colossal scale. Cervantes has Don Quixote doting on the old romances retrieved by Gutenberg; and Rabelais presents the world as a gargantuan junkheap of sludge served up for the insatiable appetites of men.

Pope's *Dunciad* proclaims the effects of Gutenberg technology first as a retriever of ancient learning and then as the agent of distraction of all learning. Saturation by ink blacked out the minds that had at first found in the printed page the "inner light." The irresistible reversal of the form whose potential had been used up brought back the cosmic dreams of *Zeitgeist* and noble savages:

> In vain, in vain—the all-composing Hour
> Resistless falls: the Muse obeys the Power.
> She comes! she comes! the sable Throne behold

Of *Night* primaeval and of *Chaos* old!
Before her, *Fancy*'s gilded clouds decay,
And all its varying Rain-bows die away.
Wit shoots in vain its momentary fires,
The meteor drops, and in a flash expires.
As one by one, at dread Medea's strain,
The sick'ning stars fade off th' ethereal plain;
As Argus' eyes by Hermes' wand opprest . . .

T

Table of Contents

THEATER

Feenichts Playhouse

> —James Joyce, *Finnegans Wake*

The seim anew

> —James Joyce, *Finnegans Wake*

A funny thing happened on the way to the Forum!

Have you heard the latest? It isn't out yet!

Michael Kirby in his study *Happenings* points out that the term "Happening" is a technical term liable to misconstruction. For Michael Kirby it refers to a kind of theater developed by visual artists, painters, sculptors, etc., and consists of environments worked up into longer forms by juxtaposition. The central feature of the Happening is the fact that, unlike scripted theater, it has no verbal matrix. In ordinary theater the actors are rigidly controlled because they program themselves upon a dialogue which may have existed thousands of years ago. In a Happening, if there is any speech, it is extemporaneous and *ex tempore*.

Kirby thinks of the Happening as completely unmatrixed, though perhaps it would be more correct to say that there is a visual or temporal frame. The events of this framework are ordered by what Miss Sontag calls "radical juxtaposition."

We notice that recent criticism takes account of the fact that Wagner's musical language (*The Listener*, November 28, 1968) is, to a very large degree, mixed with the mythic literary materials of the time. Just as the print technology, by its mental snapshotting, permits for the first time a very high degree of analytic specialism in casuistry, and the examination of the inner life, so in the case of the sciences it led to the most minute concern with precision and measurement. The word "speculation" comes from *speculum,* which meant a watchtower, not a mirror, and so meant *things at a distance.* The paradox of intense individualism resulting from the private point of view or fixed position of the new print-reader leads in the sciences to collaborative effort and teamwork in the later seventeenth and early eighteenth centuries. An outstanding example is the Royal Society. The print cliché involves not only the actual printing but the paper and other technologies. The bureaucratic organization of print cliché with uniform products and prices gives rise to capitalism as well as to the corporate activities of the scientists. This became more and more pronounced during the seventeenth and eighteenth centuries. Adam Smith and Ben Franklin are sufficient exemplars of the glorification of fragmentation applied to industry and morals alike.

Paul Goodman's *Growing Up Absurd* is a simple statement of the experience of living simultaneously in two cultures. The machine had broken the senses apart, and circuitry does the reverse. The *making* of sense ultimately has a bearing upon the cult of the absurd, and the Theater of the Absurd of the early twentieth century. When the separated or specialized senses are heavily overloaded, one tends to black out, to merge. In other words, before the development of psychedelia, intermediate projects and the Theater of the Absurd developed strategies for stimulating jaded senses or overstimulated senses. One difficulty about *making sense* in a period of very rapid innovation is that the input of the new clichés exceeds the power of human response or adaptation. When you live in a world to which you have not adapted, or had time to adapt, you "grow up absurd."

The Theater of the Absurd recognizes the fact that very rapid transitions from a specialist visual culture to integral, resonant society creates the total alienation of man. The Chinese, in their *Book of Tea,* say that the function of the artist enables us to adapt to the world we live in, and when the technological arts swamp perception and leave us no time to *make* sense, we cease to be viable human beings.

If the novelistic narrative tends to deal with the total environment selectively in the direction of creating "human interest" by means of the coincidence of motives, temperaments, and situations, the new art form of the Happening does exactly the reverse. The Happening accepts the environment, unmodified, as a colossal *Gestalt* that can be repeated, as an object for repetition and contemplation. Perhaps the newspaper is the first form of Happening. The juxtaposition of events and ads and pictures in the daily press is a world of coincidence. But little effort is applied to heighten the coincidental. Such effort is not needed. By simulating environments, the newspaper has long managed to evade attention as an art form. The fact that it is a daily product of much teamwork also serves to conceal its character as an art object. The film and photograph are also forms of corporate artistry, and the photo became an art form with the advent of film, even as film became an art form with the advent of TV.

197

The newspaper has claim to be considered the first verbal form to be subjected to the shaping power of electric circuitry. The wire services had a direct impact on the nature of reporting and relating as well as upon observing events. Telegraphic speed in relaying reports had a peculiar result upon editorial practice of laying out the copy on the page. It seems to have been discovered at once that no connection was needed between any of the events recorded. The dateline was a sufficient force to create a unified field for all events whatever. What would have happened to the story and the novel if means had been found to issue them with daily datelines? The newspaper serial with its opening "The story so far . . ." was a form that was felt more in the movie than in narrative fiction. The movie-makers found it expedient to intersperse recaps of the story every few minutes. They felt this was for the benefit of those coming into the theater at varieties of different times. Perhaps, however, the recap was a recognition of the fact that high-speed film, nonverbal narrative, can really do with additional means of unifying narrative, much as musical compositions use the recap as a basic structural means. What has been the recap procedure on TV as compared with the older film forms? One effect of TV on film has been to release it from its reliance upon story line. This, in turn, has made the recap a more integrally structural device in, say, the films of Fellini.

As an art form, the Happening does not so much address the audience as *include* the audience. It expects the audience to immerse itself in the "destructive element," as it were. At various times in the history of the theater, the audience has been included in the show to a considerable degree. In the newspaper it is decidedly the audience that *is* the show. Such, in large degree, is the nature of language. It is a Happening that includes all publics and all past perceptions in an inclusive Donnybrook of coincidences and adjustments. Once Joyce discovered language in this way, he knew he had found out the means to transform the entire human community into a work-force for the artist. Gerd Stern and the other poets of the Happening are delighted to discover that all human artifacts are available as *dramatis personae* in their theater. It is the same discovery of the "world" that has created Camp.

198

The Happening, then, is the repetition of an environment as a means of offering some control to the perceiver, for whom it is expected to be a familiar environment. An environment is far too unwieldly a thing to be usable as a probe. The art materials shaped by a single artist can serve as a probe to direct and order perception. With the Happening the exploratory and probe functions have to be assumed by the audience directly. The environment as familiar cliché is archetypalized, at least to the extent of being repeated. As in the case of the newspaper, most trivial matters are given considerable additional intensity by being translated into prose at all. That is why no account of anything can be "truthful" in a newspaper. Simply as an experience, the newspaper mention of anything alters the character of the event. All media, from language to TV, alter the patterns of perception such that all experience becomes a pseudo-event. That is why silence, as a form of phatic communion, has often appeared as a more noble kind of expression than speech: silence is golden, speech is silvern.

The Surrealist intention in manipulating the commonplace materials of the environment had been in some measure a protest against ugliness and horror. It is by no means obvious that such is the intent of the artists of the Happening. Unmistakably, however, the effect of their maneuver is to draw vivid attention to the environment as a fact worthy of attention and as one capable of being manipulated into the noblest of forms. May these artists not also sense that the invisible environment is the most invincible of teaching machines, and the most neglected?

Merely to introduce any portion of the environment into an enclosed space, or a non-environment, is to become conscious of it, and, in effect, is to archetypalize it. Again, an encounter with the environment is a kind of "Camping" out. In the world of electric circuitry, entire environments are kept in a state of interface and dialogue among themselves to the point where we will be tempted to deal with the entire world as a college campus and to program its cultures as subjects in a curriculum.

When the entire world becomes a unified and "animated collage," by virtue of the speed of information services, it is a natural step to try to deal with the entire world as a work of art. If the advent of typography and printed books inspired Machiavelli to think of the image of the Prince as a work of art, satellites and broadcasts from the moon make it quite as natural to think of the entire planet as a work of art.

199

The perception of this dialectic need not inspire disgust or enthusiasm. Such irrelevant emotions are almost certain to derive from the nostalgic discovery of derelict and banal artifacts and sentiments of the receding period. Miss Sontag writes:

> . . . If the meaning of modern art is its discovery beneath the logic of everyday life of the alogic of dreams, then we may expect the art which has the freedom of dreaming also to have its emotional range. There are witty dreams, solemn dreams, and there are nightmares.

To this one can add that consciousness, as well as dreams, has a structure that can be aesthetically enjoyed. The superior advantage enjoyed by the dream-world in the Freudian decades was that it seemed to offer a refreshing organic spontaneity in the midst of the mechanical and industrial environment. In other words, the dream-world was itself an obverse image of the mechanical world, just as Camp is an obverse image of the electric world. In Camp, one can enjoy the esoteric pleasures of Expressionism and the creative process by means of contemplation of the most vulgar objects.

The Expressionists had discovered that the creative process is a kind of repetition of the stages of apprehension, somewhat along the lines that relate Coleridge's Primary and Secondary imagination. In the same way there would seem to be an echo of the formative process of consciousness in the entire content of the unconscious. This, in turn, implies a close liaison between private and corporate awareness, though which exerts the most effect on the other may depend entirely on the degree of awareness achieved.

Miss Sontag observes:

> The Happening operates by creating an asymmetrical network of surprises, without climax or consummation; this is the alogic of dreams rather than the logic of most art. Dreams have no sense of time. Neither do the Happenings. Lacking a plot and continuous rational discourse, they have no past. As the name itself suggests, Happenings are always in the present tense. The same words, if there are any, are said over and over; speech is reduced to a stutter. . . .

The night-world of *Finnegans Wake* corresponds to this description of the Happening to a considerable degree. For great stretches of cultural time the unconscious has been the environment of consciousness. The roles of guest and host are tending to reverse at present. A century of earnest probing of the unconscious has revealed much of its structure and content, pushing them up into consciousness. Consciousness has increasingly become the environment of the unconscious until we begin to "dream awake," as it were, losing the boundaries between private and corporate. This is a revolution that has occurred more than once in the present century. For example, what James Burnham called the "managerial revolution" was the shift of power of decision-making from ownership to management. Ownership had long been the environment of the manager, but under electric conditions of information and knowledge it has become quite impossible for owners to know or to decide the great range of matters that needed hourly attention. The reversal of roles between ownership and management resulted from sheer growth in this economic sphere, quite as much as the reversal of roles between unconsciousness and consciousness is occurring at present.

Again, as the economy moves more and more into the electrical orbit of programed information, production is oriented increasingly toward service. Hardware becomes software. This process appears sufficiently in the world of advertising. As the means of advertising have greatly enlarged, the images created by advertising become an ever larger portion of the needs and satisfactions of the public. Eventually, people could look to the ad image as a world in itself, just as in poetry the symbol, when stressed, becomes much more than the content of the poem. Blake's "Tyger," for example, is a world evoked by magical incantation. Ads take on more and more of the same character.

201

The reversal of major roles in organized social action can occur almost anywhere. In the educational sphere, after centuries of stress on instruction as the business of the teacher, the entire educational process is readying itself for a flip-over from instruction to discovery. Years before he reaches the classroom, the small child of our time is engaged in data-processing on a large scale. Our schools are still arranged on the assumption that serious information is not available until the student reaches the classroom. For the child who lives in an environment constituted by information, such educational assumptions are unrealistic. Today the child, swamped by information overload, desperately needs to be taught the means of pattern-recognition for the sake of psychic survival. Pattern-recognition is the role of the researcher and the explorer. Today's young children could recover high motivation in the learning process only if permitted to tackle their environment on a discovery basis. There are many ways of doing this, but the use of small teams is indicated as essential. The same new technologies that are wiping out the boundaries between instruction and discovery are likewise wiping out differences between child and adult, so far as experience is concerned.

> What is primary in a Happening is materials—and their modulations as hard and soft, dirty and clean. This preoccupation with materials, which might seem to make the Happenings more like painting than theater, is also expressed in the use or treatment of persons as material objects rather than "characters." The people in the Happenings are often made to look like objects, by enclosing them in burlap sacks, elaborate paper wrappings, shrouds, and masks. . . .

The discovery of the materials was a reversal of roles that occurred with the Symbolists. When the painter Degas complained to Mallarmé that though he was overflowing with ideas for poems, the poems wouldn't jell. Mallarmé replied, "My dear Degas, poems are not made with ideas, they are made with words." The same discovery was made by all the arts in the later nineteenth century. Most familiar is the discovery of materials by the architects who realized that the form of a building needed to grow out of the materials used. They found that the tendency to enclose forms in materials that happened to be available was disastrous. Rather, let the available materials be the means of discovery of unique architectural forms of beauty. It was at the same time that it became obvious to artists that the medium is the message. Even as in politics and any social action, the means employed discover their own goals. Disarmament is illogical and futile, unless one is prepared to regard the available means of production and social organization as affording unique social ends. To divert electrical energy and circuitry into atomic bombs shows the same imaginative power as wiring the dining-room chairs to enable one to electrocute the sitter in the event that he might prove hostile. It is part of the age-old habit of using new means for old purposes instead of discovering what are the new goals contained in the new means.

To treat persons as material objects rather than characters is not a very accurate way of describing the Happening. It is true that in the Happening things get pushed around, just as people do in ordinary environmental life. But people enclosed in sacks, shrouds, and masks are like cartoons rather than pictures. Paradoxically, the picture is a very much more fragmentary and specialized aspect of a human being than a cartoon. The more fidelity to visual appearance the picture or image happens to capture, the more the person is imprisoned in a specialized category or classification. The "crude" cartoon, in contrast, can capture multiple facets and motivations. In the same way, the "character" in a novel is a highly specialized entity that must be kept in motion by an equally specialized story line. The story line ties events together in a quite arbitrary pattern of sequences. The modern novel began by getting the characters moving along a road in a pattern of sequential space and time. In such a pattern, coincidence in the sense of direct sequential encounters is elevated to archetypal intensity. The road as environment intensifies coincidence to such an extreme that the complexity of environmental happenings, with their many-leveled patterns and overtones, is suppressed. It is the road, or narrative, that is suppressed in the new novel or film in favor of stress on process.

203

If the narrator avoids realistic, pictorial description in favor of stylized and iconic blocs, he can include more of the environmental complexity and motivation than pictorial realism permits. This was well known to Chaucer, for example. In his time pictorial realism was a means of indicating defects of character that deprived the individual of involvement in his proper role. The character in a mask is "putting on the audience" rather than expressing himself. Thus Charlie Chaplin did not spend his life expressing his personal feelings. Like any artist, he selected from the environment of his audience the equipment he needed.

The poets select special rhythms from the great range available in the language. Chaplin chose only a small group of items: the costume of the middle-class nobody, the hidden gestures of the music-hall entertainer, the romantic outlook of Cyrano, the unlovable lover, and the foot positions of classical ballet. It was this latter inspiration that gave the bizarre highbrow aura to Chaplin's mask. Arthur Koestler tells of how, at a lavish Monte Carlo party, various people competed in simulating Chaplin's image. Among the competitors was Charlie Chaplin himself. He came in third. His failure is quite understandable when it is realized that he had to share his audience with a dozen Charlie Chaplins. Since the actor must "put on the audience," to share it is to dilute it; this is to impoverish the image, or the mask, altogether. To get into a role as opposed to merely having a job, is to put on the corporate social power of one's culture. In our still very literate society many people continue to seek corporate power by matching appearances. This has the exactly opposite effect from what is desired. It dilutes rather than enriches the experience, just as competition encourages people to resemble one another. The genuine role-player, on the other hand, doesn't have any competition whatever, since the items he selects from the environment from which to create his image are of the utmost inclusiveness. T. S. Eliot once observed that there could have been a half-dozen Shakespeares simultaneously without any overlapping or confusion of their talents. Looked at under the aspect of self-expression, a multiplicity of Shakespeares is unthinkable. All these issues recur in the dramatic strategy of Ionesco. Miss Sontag notes of him:

> Ionesco's discovery of the cliché meant that he declined to see language as an instrument of communication or self-expression, but rather as an exotic substance secreted—in a sort of trance—by interchangeable persons. His next discovery, also long familiar in modern poetry, was that he could treat language as a palpable thing. (Thus, the teacher kills the student in *The Lesson* with the word "knife.")

The point about the story of Degas and Mallarmé is precisely the new willingness to regard language as pigment, as unique material from which to create unique effects. Ionesco discovered that cliché, like the cartoon and the icon, is charged with the accumulations of corporate energy and perception. A merely private expression, or rhythm, is necessarily lacking the dimension of corporate power. The banal, as such, is rich in energy for the artist who has the skill to trigger it. To release energy in the cliché needs the encounter of another cliché! Joyce never tired of using this discovery even in its most limited verbal forms:

Loud, heap miseries upon us yet
entwine our arts with laughters low!

—*Finnegans Wake*

The Happening exploits not only the clash of one cliché against another, but also the much more effective interface of a cliché from one medium with clichés from other media.

205

NOTES ON SOURCES

Page 3. Elémire Zolla, *The Eclipse of the Intellectual*, translated by Raymond Rosenthal (New York: Funk and Wagnalls, 1968), p. 204

Page 3. James Joyce, *Finnegans Wake* (New York: The Viking Press, 1958), p. 273

Page 4. Wylie Sypher, *Loss of the Self in Modern Literature and Art* (New York: Random House, 1962)

Pages 4-5. Eugene Ionesco, *The Bald Soprano*, in *Four Plays 'by Eugene Ionesco*, translated by Donald M. Allen (New York: Grove Press, 1958)

Page 6. Friedrich Dürrenmatt, *Four Plays 1957–62* (London: Jonathan Cape, 1964), pp. 33-34

Pages 7-8. Ionesco, *The Bald Soprano*, pp. 32-34.

Page 8. T. S. Eliot, "Fragment of an Agon," *Collected Poems 1909–1935* (New York: Harcourt, 1936)

Page 8. Joyce, *Finnegans Wake*, p. 263

Page 10. T. S. Eliot, "The Waste Land," *Collected Poems*

Page 12. Zolla, *The Eclipse of the Intellectual*, pp. 215-16

Page 13. Allen Ginsberg, "Howl," *Howl and Other Poems* (San Francisco: City Lights Books, 1956)

Page 13. T. S. Eliot, "The Love Song of J. Alfred Prufrock," *Collected Poems*

Page 14. John Milton, *Paradise Lost*, Book I, lines 84-91

Page 14. *Ibid.*, lines 122-24

Page 15. Northrop Frye, *Anatomy of Criticism: Four Essays* (Princeton, N.J.: Princeton Press, 1957), p. 365

Page 15. Jurgen Thorwald, *The Triumph of Surgery* (New York: Pantheon Books, 1960), p. 285

Page 16. *Ibid.*

Page 18. Eric Partridge, *Usage and Abusage* (London: Hamish Hamilton, 1961)

Page 18. From a letter by E. S. Carpenter to Marshall McLuhan, January 20, 1961

Page 19. Graeme Wilson, *Face at the Bottom of the World*, translated by Graeme Wilson, paintings by York Wilson (UNESCO Collection of Representative Works, Japanese Series. 1969)

Page 19. Lauriat Lane, Jr., "The Literary Archetype: Some Reconsiderations," *Journal of Aesthetics and Art Criticism*, Vol. XIII, No. 2 (December, 1954), p. 228.

Page 20. W. B. Yeats, "The Circus Animals' Desertion," *Poems* (New York: Macmillan, 1957)

Pages 22-23. C. G. Jung, *Psyche and Symbol* (New York: Doubleday Anchor Books, 1958), p. xvi

Page 23. José Argüellas, "Compute and Evolve," *Main Currents* (January–February, 1969), p. 66

Page 25. W. B. Yeats, "A Coat," *Poems*, p. 148

Pages 25-26. Donald M. Frame, *Montaigne: A Biography* (New York: Harcourt, 1965), p. 83

Page 26. *Ibid.*, p. 291

Page 26. *Ibid.*, p. 82

Pages 26-27. *Ibid.*, p. 291

Page 27. *Ibid.*

Page 27. W. H. Auden, "In Memory of W. B. Yeats," *Another Time* (London: Faber & Faber, [1940]), p. 93

Notes on Sources

Page 34. Richard P. Altick, "The Case of the Curious Bibliographers," *The Scholar Adventurers* (New York: Macmillan: 1950), p. 100

Page 36. A. R. Luriia, *The Nature of Human Conflicts, or Emotion, Conflict and Will*, translated and edited by W. Horsley Gantt (New York: Liveright, 1932), pp. 422-23

Page 36. Frye, *Anatomy of Criticism*, p. 367

Pages 40-41. Edward T. Hall, *The Silent Language* (New York: Doubleday, 1959), p. 248

Pages 43-44. Mircea Eliade, *Cosmos and History* (New York: Harper & Row, 1959), p. 62

Page 44. Hans Selye, *From Dream to Discovery* (New York: McGraw-Hill, 1964), pp. 64-65

Page 44. Milton, *Paradise Lost*, Book II, lines 890-97

Page 45. Joyce, *Finnegans Wake*, p. 250

Pages 45-46. Anatol Rappoport, *Clausewitz on War* (London: Pelican Books, 1968), pp. 54-55

Page 46. *Ibid.*, p. 60

Page 46. Arthur Koestler, *The Act of Creation* (New York: Macmillan, 1964), p. 252

Page 48. William Empson, "Rolling the Lawn," *Collected Poems* (London: Chatto and Windus, 1956), p. 8

Page 49. Zolla, *The Eclipse of the Intellectual*, p. 202

Pages 49-50. *Ibid.*

Page 50. Heinrich Hertz, *Principles of Mechanics* (New York: Dover Publications, 1956)

Page 53. Joyce, *Finnegans Wake*, p. 34

Page 53. Zolla, *The Eclipse of the Intellectual*, p. 93

Pages 53-54. Eric Partridge, *A Dictionary of Clichés* (New York: Macmillan, 1966), pp. 1-2

Page 54. James Hillman, *Emotion* (Evanston, Ill.: Northwestern University Press, 1961), p. 141

Page 55. W. B. Yeats, "The Apparitions," *Poems*, p. 624

Page 56. Logan Pearsall Smith, *Words and Idioms* (London: Constable, 1925), p. 196

Page 57. George Orwell, *Nineteen Eighty-Four* (London: Penguin, 1954), p. 45

Page 59. *Poems of Gerard Manley Hopkins*, edited by W. H. Gardner (New York: Oxford University Press, 1948)

Page 60. Frederic William Maitland, *The Forms of Action at Common Law* (New York: Cambridge University Press, 1963), p. 5

Pages 60-61. *Ibid.*, p. 5

Page 61. *Ibid.*, p. 6

Page 63. T. S. Eliot, "Auditory Imagination," *The Use of Poetry and the Use of Criticism* (New York: Barnes and Noble, 1955)

Page 63. W. B. Yeats, "Sailing to Byzantium," *Poems*

Page 64. Joyce, *Finnegans Wake*, p. 227

Page 64. *Ibid.*, p. 109

Pages 64-65. Norman Mailer, *Miami and the Siege of Chicago* (New York: New American Library, 1968), pp. 88-89

Page 65. Joseph Frank, "Dostoevsky: The House of the Dead," *Sewanee Review* LXXIV (1966), p. 133

Pages 65-66. Ibid., p. 133

Page 68. T. S. Eliot, "Whispers of Immortality," *Collected Poems*

Pages 71-72. Zolla, *The Eclipse of the Intellectual*, p. 93

Page 72. Hillman, *Emotion*, p. 173

Pages 72-73. *Ibid.*, p. 289

Pages 73-74. William Empson, *Collected Poems* (London: Chatto and Windus, 1955)

Page 74. Hillman, *Emotion*

Page 74. Abraham Maslow, *Eupsychian Management* (Homewood, Ill.: Richard D. Irwin, Inc., and The Press, 1965), p. 83

Pages 74-75. Ibid.

Page 75. Hillman, *Emotion*, p. 183

Page 77. Joyce, *Finnegans Wake*, p. 561

Page 77. James Joyce, *Letters of James Joyce*, edited by Stuart Gilbert (New York: The Viking Press, 1966)

Page 81. Hall, *The Silent Language*, pp. 150-51

Pages 81-82. Peter Sypnovich in the *Toronto Daily Star*

Page 82. Jacques Ellul, *Propaganda* (New York: Alfred A. Knopf, 1965)

Page 82. George Puttenham, *The Arte of English Poesie* (London: Cambridge University Press, 1936)

Page 83. William Empson, *Seven Types of Ambiguity* (London: Chatto and Windus, 1947)

Page 83. Ibid.

Page 85. Frye, *Anatomy of Criticism*, pp. 246-47

Page 85. Ibid., p. 247

Page 85. Ibid.

Pages 86-87. Maitland, *The Forms of Action at Common Law*, p. 2

Page 88. W. H. Auden, "The Guilty Vicarage," *The Dyer's Hand and Other Essays* (New York: Random House, 1948), p. 146

Pages 88-89. Agatha Christie, *Murder after Hours* (New York: Dell, 1954), pp. 232-33

Page 90. Zolla, *The Eclipse of the Intellectual*, p. 17

Page 91. Marya Mannes, *TV Guide*, March 15–21, 1969

Pages 91-92. Peter Farb, *Man's Rise to Civilization* (New York: E. P. Dutton, 1968), p. 110

Page 92. Newsweek, May 13, 1968

Pages 92-93. Elias Canetti, *Crowds and Power* (New York: The Viking Press, 1963), pp. 373-74

Pages 93-94. Quintilian, *Institutio Oratia* (Loeb Classical Library; H. E. Butler, transl.)

Page 94. Eric A. Havelock, *Preface to Plato* (Cambridge, Mass.: Harvard University Press, 1963)

Pages 94-96. H. Marshall McLuhan, *Tennyson* (New York: Holt, Rinehart and Winston, 1956), pp. xviii-xix

Pages 96-97. Harold Rosenberg, *The Tradition of the New* (New York: Horizon Press, 1959), p. 167

Pages 97-98. Percy Wyndham Lewis, *The Diabolical Principle and the Dithyrambic Spectator* (London: Chatto and Windus, 1931), pp. 163-65

Page 99. Joyce, *Finnegans Wake*, p. 267

Pages 99-100. Puttenham, *The Arte of English Poesie*

Pages 100-101. E. Llewellyn Thomas, "Movements of the Eye," *Lasers and Light* (San Francisco: W. H. Freeman and Company, 1969), pp. 152-53

Pages 101-102. Fred and Barbro Thompson, "The Japanese Concept of *MA*," *The Saint George Dragon* (Toronto: SAC Press, 1969), pp. 6-13

Pages 102-103. Ibid.

Page 103. Voltaire, *Candide; Ou L'Optimisme*, edited, with an introduction, by Lester G. Crocker (London: University of London, 1968)

Page 104. John Locke, *An Essay Concerning Human Understanding*, edited by Alexander Fraser (Oxford: Clarendon Press, 1894), Book III, Section 1, v. 2

Page 104. Eric Partridge, *Origins; A Short Etymological Dictionary of Modern English*, 2nd ed. (New York: Macmillan, 1959)

Page 105. Leo Rosten, *The Joys of Yiddish* (New York: McGraw-Hill, 1968), pp. xiv and xvi

Pages 105-106. Ibid., p. xix

Page 108. Joyce, *Finnegans Wake*, p. 112

Page 108. Hillman, *Emotion*, p. 152

Page 109. W. K. Wimsatt, *Hateful Contraries* (Louisville: University Press of Kentucky, 1965), p. 158

Notes on Sources

Page 112. James Joyce, *A Portrait of the Artist as a Young Man* (New York: The Viking Press, 1964), pp. 252-53

Page 112. Joyce, *Finnegans Wake*, p. 579

Page 112. T. S. Eliot, "Sweeney Erect," *Collected Poems*

Pages 113-14. Edgar Z. Friedenberg, *The Vanishing Adolescent* (Boston: Beacon Press, 1964), p. 55

Page 114. Rosenberg, *The Tradition of the New*, p. 81

Page 117. Edmund S. Carpenter, *Eskimo* (Toronto: University of Toronto Press, 1959)

Page 118. Frye, *Anatomy of Criticism*

Page 119. Eliade, *Cosmos and History*, p. 5

Page 120. *Ibid.*, p. 95

Page 122. Joyce, *Finnegans Wake*, pp. 18-20

Page 123. Benjamin Franklin, notice on his printing office door

Page 126. Yeats, "The Circus Animals' Desertion"

Page 126. *Ibid.*

Page 127. *Ibid.*

Page 127. *Ibid.*

Pages 128-29. W. K Wimsatt, "Horses of Wrath," *Hateful Contraries*, pp. 5-6

Page 132. Percy Wyndham Lewis, conversation with Marshall McLuhan

Page 132. Steve Allen, *The Funny Men* (New York: Simon and Schuster, 1956)

Page 133. Rosten, *The Joys of Yiddish*, p. xix

Page 136. Joyce, *Finnegans Wake*, p. 18

Page 138. Edwin G. Boring, *The Physical Dimensions of Consciousness* (New York: Dover Publications, 1933)

Page 139. Daniel J. Boorstin, *The Image, or What Happened to the American Dream* (New York: Atheneum, 1962)

Page 139. E. R. Leach, *Political Systems of Highland Burma; A Study of Kachin Social Structure* (London: G. Bell and Sons, 1954), p. 267

Page 139. Charles Moorman, *Arthurian Triptych* (Berkeley: University of California Press, 1960)

Pages 140-41. T. S. Eliot, "Ulysses, Order and Myth," *James Joyce: Two Decades of Criticism*, edited by Seon Givens (New York: Vanguard Press, 1948), pp. 201-202

Page 141. Leach, *Political Systems of Highland and Burma*

Page 141. *Ibid.*

Page 141. Joyce, *Finnegans Wake*, p. 418

Page 142. W. H. Abrams, *The Mirror and the Lamp* (New York: Oxford University Press, 1953), p. 58

Pages 142-43. *Ibid.*

Page 143. *Ibid.*, p. 103

Pages 143-44. *Ibid.*, p. 170

Page 144. Thomas S. Kuhn, *The Structure of Scientific Revolutions* (Chicago: University of Chicago Press, 1962), pp. 13-14

Page 145. Eliot, *The Waste Land*

Pages 147-48. Eric Havelock, *Preface to Plato* (Oxford: Basil Blackwell, 1963), pp. 44-45

Page 148. Yeats, "Sailing to Byzantium"

Pages 153-54. Kuhn, *The Structure of Scientific Revolutions*, p. 46

Page 155. Douglas M. Davis, "The Dimensions of the Miniarts," in *Art in America* (November–December, 1967)

Pages 155-56. Zolla, *The Eclipse of the Intellectual*, p. 38

Page 156. Advertisement for Celanese Arnel in *The New York Times Magazine*

Page 158. William Empson, "Legal Fiction," *Collected Poems*, p. 25

Page 159. G. K. Chesterton, "The Donkey," *Modern British Poetry*, Combined Mid-Century Edition, edited by Louis Untermeyer (New York: Harcourt, 1950), p. 825

Page 160. Rosalie L. Colie, *Paradoxia Epidemica* (Princeton, N.J.: Princeton University Press, 1966), p. 3

Pages 160-61. Koestler, *The Act of Creation*, p. 94

Notes on Sources

Page 161. Colie, *Paradoxia Epidemica*, p. 6
Page 161-62. Percy Wyndham Lewis, "Vortex No. One—Art Vortex—Be Thyself," *Blast No. 1* (London: The Bodley Head, 1914)
Page 162. Colies, *Paradoxia Epidemica*, p. 6
Page 162. From a letter by James Joyce to Harriet Shaw Weaver, April 16, 1927, in *Letters of James Joyce*, Vol. I
Page 163. From a letter by James Joyce to Harriet Shaw Weaver, May 12, 1927, *Ibid.*
Page 163. Colie, *Paradoxia Epidemica*
Page 163. *Ibid.*, p. 7
Page 164. *Ibid.*, p. 8
Page 164. *Ibid.*, p. 14
Page 164. *Ibid.*, p. 13
Page 164. *Ibid.*, p. 14
Pages 164-65. *Ibid.*
Page 165. *Ibid.*, p. 15
Page 168. H. H. Watts, *The Sense of Regain*
Page 170. Michael O'Brien, "Apeneck Sweeney," *The Graduate* (University of Toronto, March, 1969), pp. 86-93
Page 170. Joyce, *Finnegans Wake*, p. 202
Page 170. *Ibid.*, p. 207
Page 172. Cartoon by Brian Savage in *The New York Times Book Review*, June 28, 1964
Page 173. Letter by Goethe to Schiller, quoted in Zolla, *The Eclipse of the Intellectual*, p. 32
Pages 173-74. Q. D. Leavis, *Fiction and the Reading Public* (London: Chatto and Windus, 1932), p. 75
Page 175. *Ibid.*, p. 29
Page 176. *Ibid.*, p. 187
Pages 176-77. *Ibid.*, pp. 33-34
Page 178. Auden, "In Memory of W. B. Yeats"
Page 179. Michael Harrington, *The Accidental Century* (New York: Macmillan, 1965), pp. 16-17
Pages 182-83. Joyce, *Finnegans Wake*, p. 455
Page 186. Cartoon by Duncan Macpherson in the *Toronto Daily Star*, October 1, 1964
Page 187. David T. Bazelon, *The Paper Economy* (New York: Random House, 1963), p. 331
Page 188. Susan Sontag, *Against Interpretation* (New York: Farrar, Straus and Giroux, 1966), p. 280
Page 195. Joyce, *Finnegans Wake*, p. 219
Page 195. *Ibid.*, p. 215
Page 199. Sontag, *Against Interpretation*, p. 271
Page 200. *Ibid.*, p. 266
Page 202. *Ibid.*, p. 267
Page 204. *Ibid.*, p. 119
Page 205. Joyce, *Finnegans Wake*, p. 259

DATE DUE

Demco, Inc. 38-293